This Far By Faith:

My Story, Secrets and All

Evangelist Lillian O. Washington

authorHOUSE®

AuthorHouse™
1663 Liberty Drive
Bloomington, IN 47403
www.authorhouse.com
Phone: 1 (800) 839-8640

Published by AuthorHouse   05/09/2016

ISBN: 978-1-5246-0839-2 (sc)
ISBN: 978-1-5246-0838-5 (e)

Library of Congress Control Number: 2016907640

Print information available on the last page.

Any people depicted in stock imagery provided by Thinkstock are models, and such images are being used for illustrative purposes only. Certain stock imagery © Thinkstock.

This book is printed on acid-free paper.

Dedication

I dedicate this book to my children and to the people who have encouraged me to put my life story in written form.

Rev. Lillian Ojetta Brown
Mrs. Ivey Irene Thompson Sanders
Mrs. Margaret Bailey-Tinsley (deceased)
Mrs. Mary G. Daniel-Wyatt

Thank you for your love, support and prayers!

Contents

A Daughter's Foreword

This book *tells* an amazing story of faith and *self-discovery*. A process that I hope you, the reader will experience for yourself, as you read through the pages ahead. It is a story of how some people heal stronger in the breaks.

My mother is one of those remarkable people.

Despite great obstacles she has bounced back repeatedly; a childhood marred by extreme poverty, mental illness, physical abuse, abandonment, illness, debilitating health issues, tragic deaths….. these are just a few of the challenges she shares within the pages of this book.

As a mental health clinician, I know that many women break or repeat the trauma they experienced with their own children but that is not my mother's story. She was determined to break the cycle and strived to create a healthy, happy marriage and family life. I'm thankful that I felt like a precious gift to my parents and learned valuable lessons, not just listening to but, watching my mother.

It's been said that a mother's heart is the child's classroom. The things that are on a mother's heart are revealed in her words and actions and they have a profound effect on her children. I'd like to share a few things I have learned from my mother's heart that have greatly influenced me. I trust that as you read this book you, too, will gain insights to managing similar problems and be encouraged that your beginning does not have to dictate your end.

My mother taught me many things based on spiritual principles, like the values of love, generosity and forgiveness. I attribute my optimism and confidence to my undaunted, always positive, ever-faithful mother.

I remember when I was 4 years old, mama gave me a quarter to put in the Sunday school offering. I did it, but I sure didn't like it. There were several other things I could think of to do with that twenty five cents.

When I got in the car to go home, I had my mouth poked out and was not very happy at all. Mama asked me, what was wrong!?! I told her that she made me give my quarter away. She said, "Honey, God loves a cheerful giver. If you give something away, you have to be happy about doing it and then God will bless you with more." I said, "He will!?!" I will never forget that. I asked for two quarters the next Sunday to give in Church. I looked for things to give away... my toys, to my friends. I have never gone without the things that I needed and many of the things that I've wanted because she took the time to explain it to me. That's how she was with me. I understood. Spiritual principles work!

My mother really wanted a daughter, someone like herself, very girly and feminine, who she could go shopping with and teach to cook and do all the things that a mother in the south would normally do with her female child. Well, I hated shopping, wasn't interested in learning to cook and I didn't like dresses. Life had certainly thrown her a curveball. She never tried to force me to be what she had expected and when others couldn't understand why, as a teen, she allowed me to wear tennis shoes with a formal dress, she simply said, "Ojetta wants to be comfortable." One thing was always clear, my mother adored me and I her. I didn't have to be her clone to be accepted by her.

At sixteen, my first semester in college, I came out to her as a lesbian. She was saddened for many reasons; yet, she never wavered in her love and affection towards me. She was and remains my example of unconditional love and grace.

There are so many stories I could relate that reveal why I think you will benefit from reading my mother's story.

I am here today as a result of my mother's faith and belief in God. She believed that by teaching me all that *she believed*, that I would know that I am never alone and that God is always with me, loving me, ready to perform the miraculous on my behalf. No, I haven't always done everything right, who has? But the words of my *mom about God's love* always come to me in my time of need. God has been faithful to answer the prayers she's prayed over the years for me and for so many others.

I will be forever grateful for the powerful and positive influence she has had throughout my life. My prayer is that I may take life's heartbreaks and transform those hits and hurts into character traits of forgiveness, compassion, kindness, and love the way my mother has.

Today, as the founder and Director of the Center for Peace and Holistic Healing, when I look into the face of my clients who may initially be broken in body and spirit, many times near death, come back to life *I am reminded of her story, her courage and I see her face.* I hear her voice as I build relationships with others and encourage them to have faith.

Because of her example I am able to see the good in people and empower them to see beyond their current situations *to* believe in themselves. I am able to provide information to help others know that they are more than the sickness or any limiting situation they are currently experiencing.

Because of her faithfulness, I am able to help others transform their mind set to "this is just a temporary situation" and to help them identify their desired outcome.

Because of her encouragement, I am able to motivate others to do the work and believe *in* the good that accompanies consistent goal oriented actions.

I feel my mother's loving spirit near when I utilize the techniques and skills I've learned and honed over the many years of practice to help facilitate restored minds, healthier bodies and renewed relationships.

My friends, my mother is one of my greatest inspirations in this life. She has overcome so much in her life to guarantee that I've had the opportunity to walk a much better path than she did. I would not be the woman I am today without her constant unconditional love.

My mother is not perfect, she remains a work in progress. She is still very much a product of her southern Christian principles, deeply devoted to God and striving to treat others as Christ would. She sees the good in everyone and sometimes to her detriment, still, puts others' needs above her own and believes everyone is entitled to a second chance.

I am sure that, within the pages of this book, you will find some experience that you can relate to. In her story I hope you will see that in many ways large and small that we are all connected and find the courage to share with others compassion, love and understanding like my mother has throughout her life's journey.

You may find yourself using some of her mottos and *words of* wisdom to help you make it through one of those times when life throws you a curve ball. You may need a shot of her brand of wisdom when someone you love tells you something you never wanted to hear. You may find words of encouragement to help you face the untimely death of a friend or loved one.

Mama has taught me, by her words and her example many spiritual principals, the most important one is "Love never fails".

My desire is that you be blessed and renewed in your mind and spirit as you read the story of my mother's life.

Lillian Ojetta Brown

Prologue

Last night as I watched the "Steve Harvey Show: Think Like a Success, Act Like a Success" he began to talk about his life. He thought that he would be a comedian all of his life. Then he began to retire from comedy and he had a game show, wrote a book, etc.

When he said he wrote a book, the Holy Spirit revealed and stated that was what I needed to do. I thought, "I do not want to write a book." It was 11:11PM on November 1, 2014, a Saturday night. I said, "I am seventy-three years old." The Holy Spirit said, "I know but the time is right."

I had thought seriously about writing a book more than thirty years ago. I did not sleep well, dreading writing a book.

At 6:53 AM the Holy Spirit reminded me of a "Word" he had given me the week before. When he gives me a prophetic word to give someone, not to dread it as I usually do, not knowing how they are going to receive it.

He reminded me to rejoice when I receive a Word for someone and even for myself. So I really tried to cheer up. I knew I had to do more than try, but to actually show genuine joy as I write this book.

At 10:18 AM November 2, 2014 Sunday morning, it was revealed to me not to share this with everyone at this time but to be very selective with whom I shared this book writing project with. Everyone does not share the belief in the things God tells you to do. I know that obedience is better than a sacrifice. So here I go asking the Lord again to help me with the writing of this book and writing it joyfully. I woke up tired and anxious.

I told my daughter, Rev. Lillian Ojetta Brown, about my experience. She was happy because she knew already and believed I should have written a book (or books) years ago. My daughter Ivey Irene Thompson Sanders would agree with her sister saying "Mother it is time for your book."

I would hear it and not hear it. After a while, I thought it was too late. But, when the Holy Spirit stated last night and this morning that 'It is time for you to write your book,' I said "I will write this book because you said so but I am not writing this book for profit." The Holy Spirit said "Yes, of course, you want to prosper from this book." I said, "Okay, you know best."

I thought how do I start a book? I have so much I could write about, so where do I start?

My daughter Ojetta said, "Mama, you just start writing." She told me to just write and I thought that is not really any help. So I picked up a pen and notebook. Not knowing where to begin, I just started writing. The words began to flow. I thought maybe Ojetta was right after all.

Lineage

I was born the first child to Lillie Lou Bush Oglesby and Jimmy Joe Oglesby in Edgefield, SC, June 12, 1941. Edgefield is in the northwest corner of South Carolina. It is the county seat of Edgefield County. Although it is in South Carolina, Edgefield is part of the Augusta, Georgia metropolitan area.

I have five siblings – James Oglesby, Joe Edward Oglesby, Cherry Oglesby Thompson, Bishop Emanuel Spearman and Effie Turner.

My Mother's Family

My maternal grandfather's name was Arthur Bush. He came from a very poor family of illiterate sharecroppers. His father was a McManus who never married his mother, Ella Bush. The reason why they never married was never really talked about but it was something that happened back in the day. He had two sisters, Ella and Mary

Arthur was a tall, slim yet muscular, dark brown skin (with Creek Indian features) very high and defined cheek bones, thick jet black hair that remained black into his nineties. He kept his hair cut short and wore a thin moustache. He helped to support his mother and two sisters by sharecropping from an early age; never attended school; could not read or write; but he could make his mark and was taken advantage of from time to time.

My maternal grandmother was named Leora Butler. She came from a more affluent and educated family. Her father's name was Henry Butler. He was intelligent and had a variety of skills. He was a blacksmith, played the accordion and was literate. He taught school three months of the year. Black children could only attend school three months of the year at that time.

Henry Butler served as the "Worshipful Master" over the York Masonic Lodge and was a deacon of Willow Spring Baptist Church. He lived to be 107 years old.

Henry's wife was Bertha. She was called Birdie and was a midwife. She could also read, was active in Willow Spring Baptist Church and died at age 57 or 58.

Leora was accustomed to nicer things. They had a nice home. She attended school and was able to read and write. She had three brothers and five sisters. They were David, Ulysses, Henry, Alice,Lanie, Frances, Louise and Leanna.

At age 18, Leora found out that she was pregnant by her brother Ulysses. The circumstances of this relationship were never discussed.

In order to avoid bringing scandal to her family, Leora seduced Arthur Bush who was 28. They lived in the same area. Leora was about two months pregnant at the time so it was a short courtship. They married shortly thereafter without him knowing that she was pregnant.

When the child was born, Leora's mother Birdie, the midwife, convinced Arthur that the child had arrived early. As the child Alvin Jack (everyone called him Stonewall) began to grow, he was the "spitting image" of Leora's brother.

This remained a point of contention between Leora and Arthur their entire marriage with the bitterness and arguments between them growing more intense as they aged. Together Leora and Arthur had four sons Uncle Stead, Uncle Robert, Uncle Johnny, and Uncle Howard. They had three daughters, Aunt Alice, Aunt Mary and my mother. They also raised Leora's sister Louise's child Willie Herbert, who we called Uncle Rooster, after her death. There were eight children in all. This is the environment my mother, Lillie Lou Bush, was born into.

III

My Daddy's Family

I did not know my daddy's side of the family like I did my mother's side of the family. I grew up with my mother's parents close by.

My father loved his family but after his mother died he drifted away from his family.

We began to travel to Bowman, GA where my dad was born when I was about six years old. Bowman is a city in Elbert County, Georgia. It is approximately sixty-nine miles from Edgefield, SC.

My paternal grandfather, Reverend Jasper Oglesby, was an assistant pastor at the Baptist church in Bowman. He could preach and sing.

He was short and stout with a potbelly. When he laughed he reminded me of Santa Claus because his stomach would shake. He had a dark complexion and was handsome.

I did not know much about my paternal grandmother. My daddy told me her name was Emma. She was very fair in complexion and a tall woman. She was a good wife and mother. She died at 48 years of age from heart disease when my father was about 12 or 13. Her death was sudden. It was rumored that she had been poisoned but that was never confirmed.

Grandpa Jasper and his wife Emma had seven children. There were two daughters Parrie Lee, and Ezzie, – one was short, the other tall. There were five sons – Linzie, Otis, John David (called J.D.), Walker, and my father, Jimmy Joe. Most of the boys were tall. My daddy was one of the tall sons and Uncle Walker is one of the shorter children.

My dad's youngest brother, my Uncle Walker is still living and was 97 on May 21, 2015. Uncle Walker has been in the hospital a few weeks with a heart condition. My daughter Ojetta and I love to visit him. He always has his television on the Golf channel. He used to play golf.

One of my uncles, Uncle J.D., was named after his father Jasper David. Uncle J.D. was a pastor in Pennsylvania. He died about six years ago and had heart disease also.

My daddy died in 2000 from cancer of the pancreas when he was 82. He was buried on my birthday – June 12th.

They called my grandfather "Jack." I called him Grandpa Jasper. About three years after Emma's death, my grandfather married again. His second wife was named Anna. My grandfather met her at a church he visited preaching. Not much is known about their courtship. She was medium build, of average looks but had no children.

My dad and his siblings told me Grandma Anna was very mean to them. They all left home early to get away from her mistreatment. My dad came to South Carolina where he met my mother.

I do remember going to Bowman to visit Grandpa Jasper and Grandma Anna. I thought my Grandpa was tall, but then I was a small child. I do recall his wife Anna was tall. She had been what they called an "Old Maid."

Lou and Jimmy

My parents came from these two very different families. But as fate would have it they found each other. My parents met in Greenwood SC. Greenwood is a small city, only 13.7 square miles in South Carolina. It is also the county seat of Greenwood County.

My dad was working for a Mr. Hayes. My dad told me that my mother was living with this lady call Mae-Mae Calhoun. He was working in Greenwood and my mother was working somewhere near there. She was 20 and he was two years older.

Mr. Hayes and my dad were out on the farm and my mother was walking somewhere when she saw him. My mother went up to him and introduced herself. Back in those times people would say she was "quite forward," now they would describe her as assertive if not aggressive. The bottom-line however was she had set her sights on my father and he was going to be hers!

At that time my dad was really interested in someone else. In fact, he was dating this lady named Eula Lagroom. She and my mother were actually dating him at the same time.

I remember my dad told me that he went to church with my mother one Sunday night, during revival. Eula was there and said that my father was going home with her. He said my mother was on one side of him pulling him to go with her and Eula was pulling his other arm to get him to go with her. Since he is my dad you know who won! My mother was very aggressive and very demanding and I guess he was afraid not to go with her.

Despite my mother claiming him for herself, my father continued to date Eula and they had a son that was born in April about two months before I was born in June of the same year.

After they had been dating for short period of time my mother told him that they were going to get married. It wasn't up for discussion she simply told him "You will marry me!"

One day she came to his job and got him. She was dressed up and told him go home and get dressed up as they were getting married that day. She told him that they were going across the street to Reverend Daniel's house and he was going to marry them. He really did not have any say in the matter.

So he went home, got dressed and they went together to the preacher's house.

It was not his idea but he said he was afraid because she was so bossy and demanding that he went along with her.

From these very different families, and this unlikely union my life, my story – secrets and all - began.

Early Life

I was born in Edgefield, SC, June 12, 1941. My mother told me she had a hard labor with my birth. She said that she crawled around all day due to the severe labor pains. My maternal grandmother came to assist with my birth. My parents were still living in Greenwood, SC but my mother came to Edgefield, SC to give birth. I was born on a Saturday evening about 5:30 P.M. weighing 13 pounds, 8 ounces. I was delivered by a midwife, Mrs. Mary Harris from Abbeville, SC. My mother stated that Mrs. Harris did a very good job with my delivery. Soon after my birth, it was discovered that I had a severely twisted foot and ankle. I was taken to the doctor and my leg and foot were tightly bandaged. The doctor showed my mother massage and exercises to do with my leg and foot in between visits. I was supposed to have special shoes, to straighten my foot and strengthen my ankle, but my parents couldn't afford them.

I was born a poor country girl. When I would laugh, my eyes would close. My mother always told me as a little girl that I had "Chinese eyes." I thought to my little self, "I am not Chinese, so why do I look Chinese?" Looking back my Grandma Emma Pledger, on my dad's side, actually my daddy's mama had very fair complexion. Maybe it was her heritage but I don't think so. More than likely my mother saw images of Asian people in magazines, books and other places and thought my eyes reminded her of them.

Not only was I born poor, I had a speech impairment. I stuttered very badly! This was from my daddy's side of the family. Not only did my father stutter but all of his siblings stuttered as well.

As a child, I knew I was born to be different than I was. Although we were poor and black I, saw images of affluence in books and magazine and had dreams of this life for myself. Even though my mother thought my dreams were farfetched they were mine and I held on to them!

I did not like being poor. I had first cousins that were born into more affluent families and that was what I wanted for myself. They lived in Edgefield. This was the home of my great uncle who owned the lumber company. I didn't feel any tension between my family and his but often it seemed like he treated us as the poor relations; but his son, William David (WD) didn't feel that way.

Had I not been exposed to some of my first cousins, seeing the difference in my lifestyle compared to theirs because they had money, most likely it would not have impacted me the way it did. It seemed like they were saying with their eyes that we, my brother and I, deserved better. I don't know how they felt. I was just glad to be there and I didn't want to leave because I liked how it felt to be there. No one knew how I felt but I felt ashamed of myself and my family.

Growing up I felt fat and ugly; my family members did not tell me I was ugly. I just felt that within myself. I was comparing myself to all my beautiful thin cousins with their new clothes which were more fashionable and looked really nice on them. They looked the way I wanted to look.

Both of my mother's parents, the Bush's, had thin lips. I noticed their thin lips because, as I remember, most African Americans had thick lips back then. As a small child, I thought, "Why are their lips so thin?"

I wanted my lips to be thin like theirs. Mine are not thick, thick but I wanted them to be just a little a thinner. Today I am thankful for my lips just the way they are.

My mother braided my hair very tightly with many pig tails or as we called them plaits. She would grease my scalp with Glover's Mange, an oil with a strong medicinal smell.

How I wanted to be slender like my brother and daddy. But I also wanted to be like my mother, but not quite as stout as she. Although my mother was stout, she had a good "figure" and shapely legs. Her clothes fit her very nicely.

She was an attractive woman. She use to say to us, "Your mother and daddy are both good looking." And jokingly say to our father, "I don't know why your children don't look better than they do."

As a child, I was often quite introspective, insecure and self-questioning about my looks and features. I thought I had the ugliest smiles. I had two smiles, one that showed my teeth (all of them) and one that only showed half of them. My first smile, that showed all of my teeth, was spontaneous and full of joy. It was unrehearsed and would burst forth when I was relaxed and happy.

The second smile was like I was crying, laughing and smiling at the same time. I would try and change my smile to one I thought was more friendly or appropriate. Although there were strong women around me they never talked to me about how to be a girl, I had to figure it out.

I sometimes wonder if, because there had been an inclination of the men in our family to sleep with the female relatives, the women in my life – my mother and grandmother especially, directly and indirectly encouraged me to be as homely as possible.

My brother, Joe was more self-confident and assured of himself. Perhaps it was a benefit of being male and sensing your power even at that young age.

My earliest memory was my mother, my brother and I walking on this high wooden bridge near my grandparents' house in Edgefield.

It was around dusk and I was scared. We had walked quite a distance to get there. I couldn't understand why we were on this bridge. We didn't know anyone in this direction. I began to cry. I thought we were going to fall through the bridge because it was old and in very poor condition. I was also afraid of the height.

My little brother Joe tried to comfort me. He put his arms around me and told me not to cry. Then he took my hand to lead me off the trestle. I don't remember our ages. We all - my brother, my mother and I – were living with my grandparents at this time. After we left the bridge everything went blank. I did not remember this event until I began writing this book. It was never discussed.

My daddy had been working in Greenwood, SC. In 1942 my dad joined the Navy. This required my parents to move to Philadelphia, PA. While he was in the Navy my father was stationed in Guam for a while.

My brother and I were very small children about 1 – 3 years of age. My baby sister, Cherry, was not born until many years later.

My mother's sister, Aunt Mary, came to stay with us in Philadelphia after my Daddy joined the navy to help my mother with my brother and I while my mother went to work and cosmetology school. I vaguely remember the house or apartment where we lived as being a dark place. I remember stumbling around in the dark trying to comfort my crying brother because he was upset and wanting his mother. Even though there were windows the shades were often pulled down. It was a very dark place.

In his absence my mother had fallen in love with another man. The prospect of her husband returning made her depressed. It was not a happy time. Her misgivings about her marriage along with the physical dark, gloominess of the apartment made for a very depressed atmosphere in our Philadelphia home.

My mother and her lover had a child together, a daughter who was adopted by her lover's sister. My father never found out about this affair or the child – a secret my mother took to her grave and was only revealed to me after her death.

After my Daddy returned from the Navy, we left Philadelphia and moved to Greenwood, SC.

While my parents stayed with my father's cousins in Greenwood, SC looking for employment, my brother and I went to live with my sweet maternal grandparents.

VI

Life with My Grandparents

The road to my grandparents' house was unpaved and dusty, about two hundred feet off the main road. The dirt road was lined by thick bushes and wildflowers. I can still smell the aroma of the honeysuckles growing around my grandparents' house.

There were no trees in the front yard but a big oak tree in the back yard. There was no grass in the yard, just dirt, which would turn muddy and sticky when it rained. In the heat of summer, we used a broom, my granddaddy made out of straw, to brush the dust neatly in place. There were chickens and a dog in the front yard.

The roof of the house was tin. The foundation was sitting up off the ground so you could see underneath the house as you approached it. The house had two entrances; you would get to the side entrance first.

There were three wooden steps that led up to the medium sized porch. There were usually five or six wooden chairs on the porch. Inside the door was the kitchen, to the left was the sitting room. It had a fireplace we used to keep warm. Behind the sitting room was a bedroom. Another bedroom was to the right of the kitchen.

There was no outhouse. We had to go out across the field to use the bathroom. It was just a field. There were no high bushes, nothing at all to provide any privacy,

In the winter I hated having to go out especially at night to use the bathroom. It was so cold. As a child I was even embarrassed to go outside to the bathroom and be exposed to someone watching me at any given time. We had no running water in the house and they had to go to the spring to fetch water.

My brother and I were so sad to be without our parents. My grandparents were trying all they could to make us comfortable and happy. My brother and I shared a bed in our grandparents' bedroom.

My brother and I were too young to fetch water and do any of the work required to keep the house running smoothly but it was hard for the adults.

It took a while, at least two weeks, for us to accept being with them; yet, we still wanted to be with our parents. We didn't want to eat at first. They told us we needed to eat to stay strong. I wondered why I needed to stay strong. They tried to cheer us up by saying our parents would soon be back to get us.

The third week our parents came to see us and brought us some nice toys. They brought trucks and cars and nice clothes for my brother. For me they had dolls, dolls' clothes and nice clothes for me too. We were so excited thinking we were going home with them to Greenwood.

My granddaddy decided he wanted to take a walk and took my brother and I with him. I think my parents told us they would be there when we returned but, low and behold, when we returned from our walk they were gone.

I was so heartbroken. I don't remember my brother's reaction. I just knew how sad and disappointed I was. I was upset with my grandparents and my parents. I was a little girl but knew this did not feel right at all to me. I did not understand how they could trick me this way. Even at my age I felt betrayed and abandoned. My brother and I wanted to be with our parents.

We had lived briefly with our grandparents before and we enjoyed being with them but our mother was with us then, before our father joined the Navy. Now we felt as if we were living with strangers.

My Grandma Leora and Granddaddy Arthur were so good and kind to us. My brother and I could not help but love them. My four uncles – Uncle Stead, Uncle Robert, Uncle Johnny and Uncle Rooster (Willie Herbert) - lived there too. They all were working in the saw mill. They all would go fishing on Friday when they got off early from work or on Saturdays.

My grandparents called me "Grand baby" and called my brother "baby boy." I didn't understand it then but my grandmother made sure to keep me a safe distance from my uncles. Given her situation with her brother, my grandmother was well aware of how female children weren't always safe in a house of men, even if they were family. There was never any inappropriate behavior from any of my uncles but trust and believe my grandmother was always vigilant.

Some mornings I would wake up to the smell of coffee percolating on the wood stove and fish, that one of my uncles had caught, frying. My grandmother would have made grits and homemade biscuits.

I use to love to watch her make up the dough for the biscuits. She had this large sack of flour and a large can of lard she used for shortening and she would add buttermilk. The flour was self-rising therefore she did not need to add baking powder and soda to the mix. They would be so good!

I also liked to watch her knead the dough once she mixed it. After she kneaded it really well then she would pinch the dough in pieces and roll and pat it into biscuits. Sometimes she would roll the dough out with a rolling pin and cut the biscuits out with a biscuit cutter. I enjoyed the biscuits either way they were made.

Other mornings I would awaken to the smell of country ham cooking. She made something called "Red Eye" gravy. It was so good over our grits. They loved their coffee and it was always one of the first things I smelled each morning.

Later in the day my grandmother use to make "Tea Cakes" for my brother and I. They were not very sweet but we loved those tea cakes. They were like a large cookie. One would fill you up.

Living with our grandparents was lots of fun, most of the time.

My grandparents had their own hogs. I remember one time my granddad was going to kill a hog. He was hitting the hog in the back of the head with an axe. Every time he hit the hog it would scream and I would scream even louder. My granddaddy called for my grandmother to come and get me. It did not help. I was still very upset. My grandmother told him he had to stop. When I went to sleep that night he and one of my uncles finished slaughtering the hog.

As a child, I did not like to see animals or humans being mistreated. I think that is what is called a "tender heart." I tried once to milk one of my grandparent's cows. When I tried to pull the cow's teat, it felt like rubber in my hand. I said "No granddaddy! I can't do this." My grand daddy had to finish milking the cow.

My grandparents had hogs, cows, dogs and chickens on their farm. One day I was out in the yard with my grandfather and a hawk flew down and got one of the chickens. My grandfather was not as upset as I was because he had seen it happen before. I wanted to get my hands on that hawk and kill it. It is the first time I recall being angry.

My brother and I were so happy living in my grandparents' home. They made us feel safe and comfortable. They seemed to have gotten along well with each other.

My grandmother had a flavoring she got from the Watkins' man. Watkin's Products were sold door-to-door and included health remedies, baking products and other household items. I did not know his name but everyone knew "THE WATKINS MAN." And cooks like my grandmother relied on him to bring a little variety to their kitchen.

She made a drink with one of the Watkins flavorings. It tasted like grape Kool-Aid. One day I decided to put some of this flavoring in the bucket my uncles used to get water from. They kept the spring water in a galvanized bucket. I put in the flavoring and the water turned purple.

I was so scared after I saw I had turned the whole bucket of water purple. I decided to go and lie down beside my grandmother while she was taking her noon day rest. She was up every morning by 5:00 A.M. to cook breakfast and start the fire in the wood stove. Around 11:00 A.M. she would take a rest plus sometimes her diabetes did not make her feel well. She would get up around 12:30 P.M. or 1:00 P.M. and start lunch and dinner.

Back to this purple water. I thought if I laid down and talked to my grandmother she would not be hard on me once she realized what I had done. She and my granddaddy were not too hard on me. They told me not to do it again if I did I would get a spanking.

My Uncle Stead had to replace the water by going to the spring to refill the bucket. He told me if I did it again he would not give me any chewing gum. Chewing gum was a big thing for me back then.

My grandparents did not spank me or my brother. We were good grandchildren. My parents would tell us to be good, mind our grandparents and not be sassy or talk back.

My brother and I played outside a lot. We enjoyed the outside. My granddaddy was in and out of the house or sitting on the porch watching us. He enjoyed watching us play hide-and-seek or rolling around old tires. Sometimes we would pull him in our red wagon that had been a Christmas gift. It was a shiny red metal wagon. One of us would push and the other would pull. It was so much fun, pure joy, to have our grandfather playing with us.

One day when my parents came to visit us my mother told my brother and I to stop pulling my granddaddy in our wagon. She said that he was too big for our small wagon. I was disappointed. We thought we were doing something great. Playing with our grandfather was such a special treat and now it was over. It had been a special time actually playing with him. After that he just sat on the porch and watched us play.

My grandparents took us to their church, Willow Spring Baptist Church, in Edgefield, SC. I remember they had some nice white neighbors, Mrs. Pearl Dorn and her family and the Timmerman family. My grandparents lived on Timmerman's land. I think their neighbor was a brother or cousin to their landlord. I think they called him Mr. Doc Timmerman. They were all friendly.

They also had some very nice black neighbors, Mr. and Mrs. Felix Kemp. Mr. and Mrs. Lonnie Gordon had an area just northwest of my grandparents place called "Gordon Town." It was about two miles from my grandparent's home.

My grandparents and uncles called my parents Lou and Jimmy. My brother and I started calling them Lou and Jimmy too. We thought we were supposed to call them that.

My granddaddy chewed tobacco. My grandma smoked a pipe. She also wore glasses which she called "specs." Sometimes she would have my brother and I looking for her glasses when she had them on all the time. She would get me to scratch her itchy scalp. This was my least favorite thing to do, then I would grease her scalp also.

I would give my grandma her insulin injections every day. This brought on my earliest thoughts of being a nurse. I did not know about nursing per say, but I felt as a little girl, that there must be a need to help people in this way.

My grandmother was a good cook. I used to love to smell the food cooking - the chicken and dumplings, fried fat-back, turnip greens and corn bread. She would cook Irish potatoes like sweet potatoes. It was so good. She also made some of the best sweet pies and chocolate layer cakes. She made potato salad with onions, eggs and vinegar. Delicious!

They had a long wooden kitchen table that seated about ten or twelve people. I enjoyed sitting around that table talking to my grandparents and eating my grandmother's wonderful meals. The table had a green and white table cloth.

These were good times but soon the day came when we had to say good bye to life with my grandparents.

VII

Back Home with My Parents

My mother had attended beauty school while in Philadelphia. When they moved to Greenwood, my mother and dad both worked for Mr. and Mrs. S. Young. My mother was their cook and my father was their chauffer. She continued to work there until she lost her vision.

My mother lost her eyesight when I was about five years old. My mother thought someone had put something in her food. She went to the doctor at one point but they could not tell her what the cause of her blindness was. The blindness came over her gradually. My mother went to a "root worker" for healing from this affliction. Consulting a root worker was common place in those days.

Shortly after consulting the "Root worker" my mother passed a long black snake. Before this day, her eyes were like blood after this incident they began to clear up but her vision was never fully restored. Some believed that the snake represented the evil that had been put in her body causing her vision problems, and passing the snake represented the releasing of some of the poison.

When mother became blind, my parents moved to Edgefield, SC and the time came for our family to be reunited. We children were living with our grandparents for about two years. This was another hard blow.

One day my Daddy showed up wearing his bib overalls and saying he had come to pick us up. I thought "why was he coming to get us?" He and Lou, my mother, were back living in Edgefield, SC and had gotten a house.

They felt it was time for my brother and me to come home. I thought "We are already at home."

By now our parents were almost strangers to us. My little mind was spinning. I thought "Why can't you and Lou live together and my brother and I stay with our grandparents?" But we had to go with them. Now I was sad to leave my grandparents who had been so nice to my brother and I. My uncles had been good to us also. But I had no choice.

My grandmother got our clothes together. I don't remember her doing this but she had to have done it as my brother and I didn't know where our clothes were. Besides we were too small to get our clothes together ourselves. I truly don't recall leaving my grandparents' home. I am certain it was tearful. I know, without a shadow of a doubt, it was very, very sad and painful. My grandparents were sad also.

My dad did not have a car. We had to walk about two miles to the house on the hill. It was a long hard walk. It seemed like five miles to me. I was like in another world. I could not believe this was happening. I do not recall any conversation on the way to the house where our mother/Lou awaited us. I felt like I was on a spaceship dreading where I was going.

The next thing I remember was that my mother was hugging me and I was not hugging her back. I do remember her smile as she embraced me. When she laughed, she had beautiful teeth and I thought she was pretty. I noticed her eyes were like a puddle of blood. I wondered, at my age, how could she smile and laugh with her eyes looking so red. I did not realize she was blind.

Later my brother and I were bringing in the wood that Jimmy (my daddy) had cut for the wooden stove in the kitchen. We called it a stove wood. Some pieces were larger than others so both of us were trying to get the small pieces of wood. Our little arms could not hold that many pieces. We did not like bringing in the stove wood. We did not have any chores at our grandparents' home.

My daddy cooked dinner. He cooked cabbage, corn and fat back. Fat back in those days was sometimes your main meat. The fat back was thick and was often cooked in oven. When it came out of the oven it would be placed on brown paper to dry it out. It would be delicious. As a child I used to like to hear the skin on the fat back crunch and crackle as I chewed it. Ham was another main meat. Certain days of the week my daddy (Jimmy) would buy fish. My daddy was doing all of the cooking, getting water from the spring and cutting the fire wood for the other stove used to provide heat.

My brother and I were trying to adjust to life with Lou and Jimmy. We were still calling them that as we had while living with our grandparents. One day Jimmy told us they were our parents and we could no longer call them by their names. He said he was our daddy. We called him Daddy Jimmy. He told us Lou was our mother and that is what we should call her – mother.

I am not sure how my brother felt about it but I did not like calling them Daddy Jimmy and Mother, not at all. I was happy calling them Jimmy and Lou. That's what I had gotten used to calling them. It almost, not almost, it did hurt my feelings to call them a name that I did not feel in my heart.

I kept on calling them Mother and Daddy Jimmy until one day it felt almost right and then one day it finally felt right. I knew then my daddy had done the right thing by telling us not to call them Lou and Jimmy anymore.

My brother Joe and I talked a lot while we were living with our grandparents. Living with our parents, Lou and Jimmy, in the beginning we did not talk to each other so much. Seems, looking back, that we were too sad to talk. We really didn't know what to say. I felt if I said anything about not wanting to live with them, it would be wrong – after all they were our parents.

Joe was a momma's boy and I was a daddy's girl. When our parents moved back to Edgefield, my daddy had to register us for school. I am thinking my brother was probably six and I was seven when I started to school. I am stating this because my brother and I went to school together. He could not start school until he was six.

Later my grandparents moved closer to us. We were so happy! We lived in a house called, "On the Hill," and my maternal grandparents lived on "the Turner Place."

My granddaddy Arthur grew some big delicious watermelons. My brother and I went to the spring to get water. From there we could see my grandparent's house. We would look up toward their house and see our granddaddy sitting outside eating watermelon.

I called out, "Hi Granddaddy!" He called back, "Hi, grand baby! Come on up and get some watermelon." We were so happy at our grandparent's home so, of course, we went to enjoy a piece of watermelon with him and our grandma. I loved them both so much!

When we returned home my mother wanted to know what had taken us so long. We told her we had eaten watermelon with our grandparents.

When we lived on "The Hill" in Edgefield, SC, my daddy tried farming. He had one mule. I enjoyed chopping the cotton. It was easy.

I would get up early and go to the field. I would chop cotton all day. I do not remember stopping to eat lunch. I'm sure I didn't. I was so proud of myself.

I do remember being sick as a child. My dad would take me to the doctor. I recall one time we went to the doctor in Edgefield at night. We went to the doctor's home. He was so nice. He examined me thoroughly. I don't remember what he told my dad about my diagnosis.

My dad worked at a saw mill back then too. Some days during the summer when school was out, I would take his lunch to him. My mother would prepare his lunch and I would walk the half mile to his job, I remember the loud sound of the saw splitting the wood.

My dad had on overalls. I didn't like seeing him wear those bib overalls but I knew he couldn't go to work dressed up. I remember telling myself, "When I get grown, I'm going to buy my daddy some nice slacks and shirts!"

My mother was a good cook even though she was blind. My brother learned to cook from her even better than I did. His biscuits looked awful but tasted so good. My biscuits looked good – smooth and nice – but tasted awful.

I remember once my mother had to have a tooth surgically extracted, she was sick in bed and her face was swollen. I decided to cook. I put on my little apron and cooked okra and tomatoes with fried fish. My mother taught me how to wash my hands and wash the meat before it was cooked. My mother was a clean cook even though she was blind.

Our house on "The Hill" was in the rural part of Edgefield. My mother made and sold fruit cakes, pound cakes, chocolate layer cakes, coconut layer cakes, caramel cakes, German chocolate cakes, sweet potato pies, coconut pies, apple pies and pecan pies. For people who did not like coconut pies she made egg custards. This was mostly during the Christmas season. I was her assistant.

For the holidays we would have turkey, ham and all the trimmings. We would have a lot of family and friends come to our home for this holiday feast. My mother made delicious ambrosia, sweet mashed potatoes in orange rind and baked so well!

Everyone knew my mother was a clean cook. Blind or not people wanted to know you were a clean cook and kept a clean house. Our house did not look that great on the outside but it was clean and well kept on the inside.

My daddy was a tall, light-skinned, slim and handsome man. My brother Joe was slim also. With mother's great cooking I wondered why they remained so slim while I could gain weight just by smelling the food.

My daddy was funny and was always making me laugh. I got my comical side from him. My mother had a beautiful smile but she seldom shared it with us.

My brother and I, in so many ways, did not have a childhood after we left our grandparents. We could not play outside like other children. If we went outside to play, mother would call us to help her.

We had a long walk to our school. We had to get up, feed the chickens and sometimes go to the spring to get water before heading to Pleasant Lane School. We would be walking to school and the school bus would pass us by. Children of our color were not allowed on the bus in those days. How I wished that school bus had been for us. After our morning chores I would already be so tired, then we had to walk at least a mile or more to school. We were already leaving home late so we arrived at school late. I was so embarrassed arriving late almost every day.

Our school teachers were family or friends of our family. Mrs. Carrie Simpkin, Miss Polly Fuller, Mrs. Parks and Mrs. Stevens all went to school to teach. We had a two room school house - grades 1-3 on one side, 4-6 on the other. Each teacher taught three grades. I loved my teachers.

On Fridays we had a program with students singing. Someone from the higher grades would come on our side and get the younger students to sing. They would laugh and make a *mockery* of us. My brother and I along with two others formed a quartet with my brother singing bass. We were a mess. My mother found out and told us not to do it again.

Her blindness limited my mother in so many ways. She was not able to attend school functions. We had to lead her around. We had to be with her when she cooked. If there was any major event we had to assist her, big time.

When we moved from the house on the hill, we moved to another house in Edgefield that was behind Pleasant Lane Baptist Church. We could not cook on the stove. The first time we tried to cook inside, the house filled with smoke. I ran outside and saw all the fire coming out of the chimney. I was so scared. I started yelling. I don't remember what happened next. I do know we had to cook on the outside. My daddy was in Greenwood, SC working.

My daddy soon got us a house near an affluent neighborhood. The evening we moved I saw this old ugly shack and I thought "Who lives there?" Then we turned off the main road and headed away from the affluent homes in the direction of the shack.

I thought, "Oh no, we are moving here!" This house was in no condition for anyone to live in; yet, we were moving there. It was a shameful place to live! It looked like it should have been condemned. Some of the wood in the house was old and rotten. In the kitchen the floor was so bad you had to be careful not to fall when going from one end of the room to the other. There were five rooms and a bath.

I was twelve when we moved into this shack and Joe was ten. Little did we know that our family was about to grow as my mother was pregnant with my sister Cherry. I could not tell if my mother was happy about this pregnancy.

Before her birth, I wanted a sister. My brother Joe wanted a brother. Cherry was born at the Brewer Hospital. Brewer was the hospital for African Americans. Dr. Walter Bishop, Sr. was the attending physician.

My sister Cherry was brought home to this same shack after her birth. Daddy came home one day and told us we had a little sister. I was so glad. I felt superior to my brother. Now there were two girls in our family.

I came up with a name for our little baby sister. My name was Betty Jean and Joe's name was Elaine. When my mother and the baby arrived home, she had named the baby Cherry Arthur Lee.

I thought, "What kind of name is that?" My mother told us she had a friend in Philadelphia, PA that had a cute little girl named Cherry. She had decided if she ever had another girl she would name her Cherry. I asked my mother where the Arthur Lee came from. She said Arthur was for her daddy and Lee was for her mother, Leora. My brother and I were disappointed but I did like the name Cherry right away.

When my mother gave Cherry a bath she would cry. As soon as the bath was finished, my mother would put baby lotion by Johnson & Johnson on Cherry. The lotion was pink and smelled nice. After my mother had put the lotion on her and dressed her Cherry was ready to be fed. My mother breastfed Cherry then she was ready for her nap.

Cherry was one month old when my Uncle Johnny was killed. I was so sad. As I said before, he was my favorite uncle. This man named Fred Mack shot him in the back.

Uncle Johnny was dating Mack's step-daughter. And, from what I heard, Fred Mack was liking his step-daughter also. Uncle Johnny was only 23 years old. He was such a nice guy and so handsome!

When we lived in the house in Edgefield, where we had to cook outside, Uncle Johnny always brought us food and fresh watermelon and gave us money. The other uncles were nice too, but Uncle Johnny was the best. When I was a little girl I used to say if he was not my uncle, when I grew up, I would marry my Uncle Johnny. I stated that to myself.

We stayed in this shack for about a year. Finally after my mother's complaining and my pleading my father moved us to a house in Greenwood, SC on Hackett Street. It was much nicer than we had been living. It was roach infested and needed cleaning but after extermination, it was a step up. We had been living there, not quite a year, when I turned 15 in June. That September my father left our family.

Cherry was three years old when my father left our family. He gave no indication that he was going to leave us. His employer Mr. Brooks called that afternoon about 2pm and wanted to know if my father had gotten back from the doctor's visit with my mother. I told Mr. Brooks that my mother was sick. I told him that she should be taken to the doctor but my dad left at 7 AM and we had not seen him since then.

It was Labor Day when he left. We did not know where he was until a week later. That was a stressful week to say the least. He left in the new car that my mother had purchased about six months prior. It was a beautiful blue and white Buick.

A week later he called and said he was in Baltimore, Maryland. I knew he wasn't coming back because my mother was so abusive to him. I was glad for him but I was sad for me. Cherry didn't seem to notice her father was gone, but I missed him terribly. My brother Joe left shortly after my father left because he was tired of my mother's abuse also. Joe moved to Edgefield and started working with our cousin, WD who was a pulpwood producer.

My parents' relationship had never been easy. My mother was very jealous and was physically abusive to my father. If he was even fifteen minutes late coming home from work, my mother would have gotten out her gun. When they sat down to eat sometimes it would be with the gun on the table. If he went outside to get wood for the heater and took longer than expected, she would shoot up in the air. I had even seen her throw my daddy to the floor and sit on him. I guess he had finally had enough so he left us and went to Baltimore, MD.

My daughter Ojetta for many years had not had a relationship with her grandfather. When she confronted him about his abandoning his family he explained the abuse and violence in the home he had experienced at the hands of her grandmother. He explained his fear had prompted him to leave. No one had ever asked him his side of the story. It had been a heavy weight on his heart and after he and Ojetta talked he said it was like a thousand pound weight had been lifted from his shoulders.

My daddy Jimmy Joe sent money back to support us from Baltimore. He wanted us to be cared for but he just could not live with my mother any longer. Although I was just a teenager I went to work, sometimes working three jobs. I worked for the Daniels and the Crimes families.

They were affluent and treated me as a part of the family. Even though they were white and I was a little African American girl, I believed, from seeing how they were as a family, that somehow I could have a happy family one day. I believed that I could live in a gorgeous house in a lovely neighborhood with beautiful things too.

The Daniels helped me to believe I could have and experience a life better than I experienced at home. Seeing and being in that environment, being accepted and being loved let me know that there was a better way to live and I could be a part of it.

But at home, I would give all the money I made to my mother to help support our household. Mother did not blame us for father's departure because she knew in her heart that she was to blame.

When I was seventeen, I noticed a nice man living in our neighborhood. He was a truck driver. I had seen him driving a huge eighteen wheeler truck for Wilson Brothers Sand and Foundry Company.

He was tall, about 6' 6", muscular and dark skinned. He was always a gentleman and so kind to everyone he encountered. I thought he would make a nice friend for my mother. I told each about the other and they agreed to meet. His name was Lewis Wardlaw.

After their initial meeting they dated for about a year. Lewis wanted to get married but mother did not. They decided that he would move in but he was never able to persuade her to get married again. He was a good humored gentleman and an excellent provider. We called him Pop Lewis. He loved us and we loved him. Pop Lewis functioned in every way as a father to me and as a grandfather to my children. He was with my mother for 18 years, until her death. During her illness, I talked to her about the plan of salvation and she accepted Christ. She was so happy to receive the promise of salvation.

VIII

A Childs Dark Secret #1: When My Daddy Was Inappropriate

That ugly shack brings back many unpleasant memories and a horrible experience I must reluctantly share.

The lady we were renting from, Mrs. John Coleman, had a friend that needed a night nurse, someone to stay with her child for a few nights while they went on vacation. Mrs. Coleman asked my mother if she could do it. My mother said yes.

While mother was away all night, my daddy woke me up and asked me to go with him. I followed him into the living room. We sat on the sofa.

He put his arm around me and asked me how would I like for him to put his "candy stick" into me? I pretended I was so sleepy I could not wake up. Then he said, "The reason I am asking you this is because you are getting to the age boys will be asking you this."

I was still pretending to be very sleepy. It seemed like a nightmare. Then he said, "You are a good girl. Go back to bed!"

I thought, "Did my daddy just do this?" YES, he did!

The next morning when my mother came home my daddy had already left for work. I told her what had happened.

She called him at work. He came home and they had a big blow out. My mother told Mrs. Coleman to tell her friend she would not be back to work for her. My daddy never tried it again.

I was in denial for a long time but now I know he was speaking about himself that night. Having sexual contact with a relative seemed to be common place – even with your daughter. I did not mention it to him. I was in complete denial. Actually, I had repressed the memory. It was so deep in my subconscious mind that I didn't think about it. If I did think about it, I would say to myself, "It didn't really happen." I only wish I could say that; but I can't.

Ironically, not at any time did I feel threatened by my daddy. He did not move his hand off my shoulder. Before and after that incident he was always a loving father. He called me his "little girl" from the time I can remember to the day he died.

One day later in life, when I was in my 30's, I said, "Daddy, I am not a little girl anymore." Daddy replied, "You are my little girl and you always will be."

Writing about this I had a flashback. My daddy said to me at that time "I need to clear up something." I said, "What is it daddy?" He said, "I need to ask your forgiveness about the time I asked you an inappropriate question. Do you remember?"

I said, "Daddy I had forgot about that."

He said, "Daughter, I have not forgotten. Daddies are supposed to protect their daughters. Will you forgive me for asking you something like that?"

I said, "Daddy you are already forgiven." We both had tears in our eyes.

Writing this book - that the Lord said to me, it is time for me to write – has brought to the surface so many things that have been embedded way down on the inside. Thank you, Jesus for reminding me that my daddy did finally apologize.

IX

A Childs Dark Secret #2: Mother's Abuse

My mother could be abusive. I did not want to write about this. It is something you don't want anyone to know about - that it has happened or is happening.

It is so embarrassing to admit that your mother whipped you until your legs bled or made you pull off your clothes then beat you until you had whelps all over your body. I could not believe my own mother treated me this way.

I remember one time when my mother had this beautiful watch. I always liked beautiful and fancy things. I got the watch out of the drawer where she kept it, put it on my wrist and wore it into town. Somehow I lost the face of the watch. I came back home and put the watch back into the drawer not realizing the face had fallen off.

That Monday my mother realized the face was missing from her watch and one of us must have worn it. She called my brother and I home from high school around 1:30PM. I was in my teens. When we got home she told us to pull our clothes off because she was going to beat us until we told her who had worn her watch. I told her I had worn the watch to town on Saturday to order groceries. She told me to pull off my clothes and lie across the bed. She got her long thick belt and beat me something awful.

That day I had to go to the Daniels' home to babysit. I always went there directly from school as someone would pick us up at the schoolhouse. But that day, because my mother had called us home, I had to walk to the Daniels'. It was a very long ways to walk. As I walked I asked myself did I deserve a beating like this. Shouldn't discipline be firm but loving? Shouldn't a parent tell their child "What you did was wrong and you are going to be punished," not try to beat them to death?

When I got to Mrs. Daniel's home, she said, "Irene, what happened to you?" I had practiced all the way there, as I walked, what I would say. I told her while I was in biology class, the assignment had blown up and put all these bruise marks on my arms. Thinking about it now, I doubt that she believed me. I believe she may have called my mother and asked what had happened to my arms.

My hands were also covered with bruises so I kept them under my stomach. Mrs. Daniel couldn't see the bruises on my back and I wasn'tgoing to tell her lest I get another beating from my mother.

When Dr. Daniel came home he asked to see my arms. He said he did not believe my biology project had blown up. He said if there had been an explosion there would have been bruising on my face and chest. He asked me again what had happened but I only repeated my story of the biology explosion.

Mrs. Daniel was very upset by the bruising. I didn't let the children see the marks from the beating. I would not have been able to explain to the older children Mary G. and John. The youngest Lambert (Bert) was too small to notice.

Dr. and Mrs. Furman Daniel were like parents to me. They actually called me their adopted child. Mrs. Daniel would tell everyone, with pride, that she helped raise me. They encouraged me to believe that I could have a better life. She taught me proper etiquette and how to entertain guests. I saw how they lived; beautiful house, new cars, nice clothes, etc.

They treated me like a part of the family. Mary G and John always treated me like their sister. Lambert was only a few months old when I entered their lives. He was six when I left. The youngest son, Russell, was unborn.

The Daniel's home was like a safe haven to me but I felt too ashamed for people to know what I was going through. I do believe Dr. and Mrs. Daniel did talk to my mother as it seemed the abuse lessened after this incident.

I didn't feel I had anyone I could talk to in confidence. I thought maybe it was my fault or can I trust anyone with this information. I am sure if I had had someone to talk to, I would have; but I felt too ashamed. I thought people might not like my mother if they knew she beat me.

My mother was not always this way when we were living by my grandparents. It started when we were preteens and continued through our teen years. It seemed that she hated me for a while.

I still don't know what that was about. I thought bipolar depression or other mental conditions. I thought maybe she was angry with me for living and thought since she couldn't abort me, she would beat me to death. I don't know only God knows.

My daddy knew about the abuse but he was afraid of her. Yes, he was understandably afraid of her but I still thought he was a coward not to confront her and put a stop to her abuse of my brother and me.

I favored my daddy over my mother because he was kind to us. He never struck us, not once. He did chastise us if we misbehaved but with love. Maybe I was wrong for calling my dad a coward. My mother was very strong.

My daddy left when I was fifteen. He could not take the abuse any longer. I was devastated when he left. I knew he was afraid and needed to be safe, therefore I couldn't blame him. But I couldn't help thinking he had left me here with this crazy woman. When he was there he hadn't done anything to protect us, so he might as well have left.

Somehow I knew the Lord was not going to let this separation from my father be until "death do us part" and at some point he was going to protect me.

So my dad left but he did send financial support. It wasn't the same as his presence but he was still supporting his children, he cared. How I missed my Daddy! He moved to Baltimore, MD and later remarried. I didn't like his wife. I felt like she had taken my Daddy from me. The truth is my mother was at fault not my daddy or my stepmother.

After I got married, my mother began to take out her anger and frustrations on my sister Cherry. One day she called me and told me Cherry was a few minutes late from school. I tried to call her again later but got no answer. I knew Cherry was getting a beating. I drove over to my mother's house – a five minute drive. I knocked on the door and no one answered so I broke the door in.

Cherry had on no clothes and mother had been beating her. I told my mother not to strike Cherry again. I told her if she hit Cherry again she would have to deal with me. I believe in honoring your parents but this abuse was terrible.

I told Cherry if our mother told her to take off her clothes again she knew a beating was coming. I told her to run out of the house, clothes or no clothes, go to the neighbors and call me. I promised her I would come and pick her up day or night.

I turned to our mother and said, "If you can't treat your daughter Cherry, my sister the right and loving way, she can come and live with me." I told her I thought she had mended her ways about beating her children.

I believe my mother had to have a mental illness of some kind to beat her own flesh and blood this way. I could never do this to anyone's child regardless of the situation. How could your heart allow you to be so mean?

I did not have a protector, because no one knew I was being abused. I did not tell but I knew my mother's pattern and I had to protect my sweet little sister, Cherry.

I asked my mother if she loved me. She stated that she did. I asked her why she had treated me the way she did – I didn't understand. She began to cry and said she didn't understand it either.

At that point I felt sorry for her. My mother and I became closer. It was a process. I didn't really know if I could trust her. Later on, I guess about a year later, she began to treat me like a mother treats a daughter with love and laughter. We began doing things together such as shopping, cooking, inviting family and friends over to dine with us. It was a pleasure.

As our relationship healed, we grew closer. My friend's came to love her as well. We would have something called "Socials" back then. I would invite my friends over from school and church. My mother would cook some good food. We would play records, dance and eat.

My mother loved to cook. Everyone would praise her cooking. Mother would smile and appreciate it. I was bubbling with pride and joy my mother had come home at last!! We would enjoy getting dressed up and going to church together. My mother loved her grandchildren and treated with so much love and kindness. I think she was trying to make things right by her own children with her love and affection for her grandchildren. She would go all out for them.

We never talked about the abuse with our friends and family. I believe after my sister's tragic death, my mother's heart continued to soften.

I am so thankful to God that I finally had the experience of having a kind, sweet and loving mother.

I am telling my story, hoping and praying it will give someone else the courage to do the same. You cannot imagine how much strength it took for me to tell the truth about how my own mother abused me but it needed to be told. I needed to share my experience for me. It has somewhat crippled me by not sharing this.

I thank and praise God for changing my mother so I can relate and remember some wonderful times with her. I will always cherish those times but from time to time the memories of the beatings come up. I see the scars on my arms. They are almost faded now but I can still see them.

I pray and cancel the thought of the pain from the beatings. I ask the Lord to help me forget. I continue to thank God for the love and forgiveness toward my then mean mother to the loving, kind and sweet mother she became.

X

Gone too soon: My Beloved Sister Cherry

My father was a loving kind father to all his children. That love extended to the newest addition to our family Baby Cherry. He would pick Cherry up if she wasn't asleep when he came in from work. If she was asleep, he would have dinner and pick her up later. I can remember my father playing with Cherry and she would be laughing and jumping.

Even though he was disappointed because he had wanted a little brother, my brother Joe was happy with his new baby sister, Cherry seemed to have really liked her brother. She would always smile at him when he would play with her.

Cherry was a very friendly and happy child. Although she didn't like baths as a baby, when she got older she would splash and play in the water. Cherry enjoyed being around people, especially me. I say that she enjoyed being around me because when I came into her presence or vice versa she would light up, always smile and be just jumping and reaching for me. At this time, mother was blind but she could see enough to take care of the baby.

Cherry was three years old when my father left our family. Cherry didn't seem to notice her father was gone, but I missed him terribly. I loved having a little sister. I told her that she was a sweet girl and that she was beautiful all the time. She would be so happy and just grin from ear to ear. I would always say, "Come here and give me a hug girl!" she would reply, "Rene, you love to hug!!" We gave each other lots of hugs.

I registered Cherry for school when she was six years old. Cherry went to East End elementary school. Cherry really liked school. When she would get home from school she would be excited about what had happened in the classroom. She would talk about her teachers and she would talk about her friends.

As she got older, Cherry would say, "Rene, do you think you are beautiful?" I told her that I don't know if I'm beautiful, but I think I'm pretty. She said, "Well, l know I'm beautiful!"

She loved to dress up and go to school. I helped her to have the clothes and things she needed to help keep her self-esteem high. We had long talks about how to take care of herself and to feel good about herself.

Cherry was very feminine and she liked girly things. She would stand in front of the mirror and fix her hair in different styles. If she did not like that style she'd change it to another style and then she would beam. She would twirl around and say "I'm so beautiful!" I would say, "You are!" and she would just laugh and be happy. Cherry liked to get in front of the mirror and primp and preen. She knew she was beautiful.

I got married when Cherry was six years old. My husband Norman loved Cherry so much and she loved him too. She called him Brother Norman and he called her Sis. Cherry stayed at our house a lot because I would go pick her up.

When Cherry first saw my baby Ojetta, she was so happy. Cherry acted like she had a baby sister. That's how she initially just fell in love with Ojetta. She was so happy. They made each other laugh and got along beautifully right from the start.

When she was not at our house, often Ojetta would be over there at my mother's home. After work I would go pick both of them up. I would cook dinner and some time we would go out to eat at Burger King or McDonald's. We had a lot of fun together and enjoyed being together.

My sister Cherry and my daughter Ojetta were so very close. They were more like sisters than aunt and niece. They loved each other so much. Cherry could comb Ojetta's hair and it would look so nice. When I combed Ojetta's hair it would look like it needed Cherry do it over again. I remember one day it began to look stormy. Ojetta wanted Cherry to comb her hair standing on the front steps so she could watch the sky. I thought that was so cute. Cherry and Ojetta got along with each other so well.

My mother was not abusive to Cherry at all while I was in the home. As Cherry became a teenager she wanted to socialize and spend time with her friends as any teenager would. She loved to talk! My mother gave Cherry a very hard time.

She made it very difficult for Cherry to spend time with children of her own age. When Cherry was about thirteen years old, she was 15 minutes late arriving home from school. Mother brutally beat her with a belt. I was unable to reach my mother via the telephone that day. Something just told me that she was beating Cherry. I broke all the speed limits and tore the door off the hinges getting inside to stop the beating. I angrily told my mother that if she ever hit Cherry again, l would take Cherry to live with me forever!!

After that incident, I made it a point to have Cherry at my house often so that she would feel the love and warmth of the family. She was able to socialize with children her own age in the neighborhood. She was such a bright and outgoing girl with many friends at school.

Cherry had just turned 15 when she met Norman Thompson at school, he was 17. She was not allowed to date, yet they fell head over heels in love with each other. They only saw each other at school and spent some time on the phone talking. After about six months after they met they decided to get married.

No one wanted them to marry – not my mother, his family, nor I. We all talked at length about it. I wanted Cherry to go to school and become a nurse. She promised me that she would do that later.

Norman and Cherry convinced everyone that they belonged together - RIGHT THEN - no waiting! Somehow they felt it. They knew how precious time was and how little of it they would have together.

Even though there was a seven year difference in Ojetta's and Cherry's ages, (Ojetta was an old soul) they were the best of friends. On March 28, 1968 Norman and Cherry took Ojetta with them to be married at the court house. Norman had just turned eighteen on March 26th.

They had their son Norman Thompson Jr. (Chip) on January 12, 1970 and their daughter, Ivey Irene Thompson on December 29, 1970.

My sister Cherry was killed in an automobile accident Monday, August 28, 1972 just two days after her 19th birthday when an intoxicated man, driving on the wrong side of the road, hit their car head on.

Her son Norman Jr. (Chip) was two years old and her daughter Ivey was only one when she died. Both were in the car with her. Chip was in the hospital for three days and Ivey for five days. Ivey had seven stitches in her head. Their father Norman Thompson Sr. was in the hospital for three months.

When Cherry was killed, she and her family were on their way to visit our mother's home in Greenwood, SC. They lived in Ninety Six, SC.

I had seen her and her family on Saturday night when she had come to get her birthday presents. Cherry wanted me to purchase her some Tupperware which I did. I also gave her a monetary gift.

Back then people were wearing hip-huggers. Cherry had on her hip-huggers and so did her daughter, Little Ivey Irene. She was walking and looking so cute, I had to laugh at her. Ivey always had a sweet smile, so did her mother.

Her husband, my brother-in-law, was taking Cherry and their children to the movies to celebrate her birthday. I have always been big on birthdays.

Cherry thanked me so much for her birthday gifts. She said, I can still hear her now, "Rene you are always doing something nice for me and I can't do anything for you." Cherry called me Rene, my nick name.

I said, "Oh honey, don't worry about that, your time will come" - not knowing it would be one of the last times I would see her alive. Actually the last time I saw her was the following Sunday. She had picked up her birthday gifts the Saturday before.

My sister always cooked dinner for me on Sunday when I had to be on duty from 7AM-3PM. So she came that Sunday, dinner usually ready or almost ready when I got home about 3:30 or 3:45PM. This Sunday the dinner had not really started, she had the green beans cooking and had made a tossed salad. I came in, took a shower and helped fry the chicken. I made the gravy. Cherry cooked the rice and corn bread. I had made lemon pies the night before and iced tea.

Cherry had been outside talking to our next door neighbor. We sat down to eat about 4:45PM. The food was so delicious or maybe we were just so hungry.

Cherry was so friendly and loved to talk. Her children Ivey and Chip like to talk too.

After viewing my sister's body I went to the pediatric unit to check on Chip and Ivey. Chip was asleep but Ivey was in a playpen beside the nurses' station. As soon as she saw me she jumped up smiling jumping and laughing. I picked her up into my arms and held her close to me while my heart was breaking. While their father was in the hospital Chip and Ivey were with me or Norman's mother most of that time.

The driver of the car that had hit my sister that sad day was also hospitalized. The passenger in his car, his girlfriend, was also killed in the accident.

When I returned to duty at the hospital I found the young man that ran into my sister and her family's car was a patient on my floor and was actually assigned to me.

I went in to speak to him. He was smiling. I could tell he was in a mood to flirt. The smile soon faded as I introduced myself. He apologized and said how sorry he was especially for his girlfriend. I did not appreciate that statement. I told my head nurse, Mrs. Herlong, that I could not deal with him. I think my friend Viola Carroll became his nurse.

When Cherry was killed, my daughter Ojetta became depressed and just wanted to lie on the sofa and watch television. I was depressed too.

I have not dealt with my sister's death as of yet. I have not had time to grieve.

After Cherry's death, Ivey and Chip looked to me as their mother figure. Initially after Cherry's death, when Chip and Ivey would call me "mama" I didn't want them to do that because it reminded me of why they were calling me that.

I remember when my husband Norman would come home from work, take his work boots off and put on his bedroom slippers, Ivey what climb into his shoes. She would drag around in his big shoes with the widest grin on her face. I would tell her, "Darling you are going to hurt your little legs trying to pull those shoes around". My husband would say, "Sugar babe, I think She's gonna be all right." She looked so happy and proud, I let her do it for a little while.

Cherry's husband Norman eventually remarried. We remained very close with him and his family, picking Chip and Ivey up on the weekends and often they spent the entire summer with us. They were my children too and I was their mother. Ivey came to stay with us the summer she was going into the 11th grade. Chip had moved to his uncle's home the year before.

After Cherry's death, her daughter Ivey and I became very close, so close that I came to feel that she was my child. She is much more than a niece. When I speak of Ivey, I now refer to her as my daughter; I adopted her.

I have not dealt with my sister's death as of yet. I have not had time to grieve.

Adult Life

Marriage to Norman Brown and Starting My Family

I married Norman Brown when I was 18 years of age, almost 19. He was 38. He died at age 51 when I was 32. He had suffered for years with gastritis and stomach problems. I had to cook his food a certain way and he took medication to soothe his stomach.

Norman's first wife had died. His first wife's name was Margaret. We all went to the same church. Margaret sang in the young adult choir. She was dark complexioned, kind of short, kind of stout but shapely. She had a nice smile and was very friendly. She and my mother were good friends. They lived close to us until they purchased a new home and moved 5-7 minutes away. I knew them as Deacon and Mrs. Brown.

They had a sweet precious son named Harry. I knew Harry, who later became my step-son, since he was a baby. They trained him well. He had very good manners. His father called him "Cap" because he loved to wear caps. Harry was almost eight years old when I married his father.

Harry was adopted when he was an infant. He had a twin named Larry who was adopted by another family – Mr. and Mrs. Moore.

Some years later Mrs. Brown became ill. I think she had cancer. People said that Deacon Brown took very good care of her. She died approximately three years after being diagnosed.

After her death Deacon Norman Brown had ladies calling him and coming by his home. One day after church services he asked if he could come and see me. I told him maybe and I would let him know.

I told my mother that Deacon Brown had asked if he could come and see me. My mother and Mrs. Brown had been good friends. I asked her if Mrs. Brown had complained about how she had been treated in her marriage to Deacon Brown. Mother stated she always told her he was a good husband and father. That made me feel better, so much better.

I had my eye on Deacon Brown and so did many others. He did not know that I was interested in him. I was playing it real cool. I knew him from church. He was always friendly, respectful and kind. But I was not going to be in a contest with these other women.

He asked me a few more times about coming to see me. I finally told him ok. So he would come to see me after church on Sunday evenings, then we were having church services from 5-6:30PM. He and his son Harry would come by afterwards.

One evening Harry said, "Tell her daddy! Go on and tell her." Harry was always so precious. I said tell me what. Norman said he wants you to know Mrs. So & So came by the house. I said, "Oh yeah?" I told Harry, "Son, your daddy knows what he wants to do. But I am not going to be in his game plan." Norman said, "Oh this is not a game. I know who I want and it's you."

One day he told me he had gotten me a stereo system, that's what we called them then now they are called Entertainment Centers. I asked him where it was. He said it was at his house. I asked him why my stereo was at his house. Then he got down on one knee and asked me to marry him. He had this big diamond ring. By then I was truly in love with Deacon Brown and his son Harry.

Before we were married Deacon Brown asked for approval from my mother. My mother told him to treat me like he had his first wife with love, respect, kindness and appreciation. She told him if he didn't he'd have to answer to her. I thought is this the same mother!?! Thank you Jesus!!

Norman was tall with a dark complexion, handsome, friendly and kind once the alcohol was removed. He loved his family. He loved to surprise me with clothes, furniture, diamonds and even a new car once.

When we got married I was three months pregnant. We went out the first time and it happened. We used protection and I wondered how this had happened. Norman told me later he had pinched the tip of the condom because he wanted me to become pregnant. Well, I thought I wanted children but had planned on the marriage then children. We both were happy.

I knew people were going to talk about us – the Deacon and the Secretary of the church – pregnant before marriage. I knew tongues were wagging. My husband said, "Sugar Babe, don't worry about people. They talked about Jesus and he did no wrong." I told him, "Yes, but Jesus is stronger than I am." He laughed and said, "God is a strengthener and he is a forgiver." My husband was a praying man. I always wanted a husband that was a Christian and a prayer warrior. He was both.

We declared that we were having a healthy baby girl. I had always wanted a son first and then a daughter. We already had our son Harry, so now we were expecting a daughter. We did not have ultrasounds back then to tell the baby's gender. I spoke it by faith. When we told Harry we were pregnant he was so happy. He wanted a baby brother to play with even though I was saying I was having a daughter.

I had my son Harry and now I had to get ready for the arrival of our baby girl. As I said before I was three months pregnant when Norman and I married.

My neighbors were friends with my husband and his first wife. Some were mad, and maybe jealous, because I was pregnant. We had gotten married just six months after Mrs. Brown had died which in some people's minds was too soon. Norman and I did not start talking until after Mrs. Brown's death, yet the relationship, developed quickly after I agreed for him to visit me. I felt it was too soon to marry too. Norman and I were quickly engaged, but the pregnancy prompted us to get married sooner than we had planned.

The neighbors were still grieving, so was I. I am sure my husband and son, Harry were still grieving too.

Everyone was pretending they were alright with our marriage and also the fact that we were pregnant. I didn't know that people could be so fake; hiding how they really felt. As my pregnancy progressed, I had health issues and I did notice some of their attitudes toward me changed for the better.

No one gave me a baby shower so I went to town and purchased my own baby clothes. I got all pink. I said if the baby was a boy, he was going to wear pink. I knew in my heart that the baby was going to be a girl.

I remember one day we were over my mother's home. I was sitting in a chair in the living room. I got up out of the chair and went into the kitchen where my mother was cooking. My sister Cherry went into the living room where my husband was sitting.

When Cherry sat in the chair, that I had been sitting in, the chair fell down in pieces. I was about seven months pregnant. Everyone was so happy that I was not in that chair when it fell apart! It was a miracle.

Cherry was about six years old. She thought my pregnant figure was due to eating too many hot dogs and hamburgers. I told her I was having a baby and that was why I was so fat. It wasn't hamburgers and hot dogs but I did have a craving for watermelon while I was pregnant. Sometimes I would just open the refrigerator and look at it. Now I have no desire for watermelon at all.

By my eighth month of pregnancy I was visiting the doctor every week. My doctor, Dr. John Harrison decided that because of the way my pelvis was made, I could not deliver a baby vaginally. He told my husband and I that I would have to deliver by C-section, for my safety and that of our baby. When my husband heard the news he just cried and cried. He did not want me to have surgery. Later the doctor told us I could only have three caesarean sections. I had always wanted five children.

Six months after our wedding we had this 8 pound 5 ounce baby girl, Lillian Ojetta, a little butter ball. We loved her so much. Her head still looks the same only bigger! Harry had a little sister and she had a big brother. She was so beautiful.

Ojetta started to walk at eight months. She had a baby walker. In no time she was all over the place. You had to get out of her way or she would run right over you. Everyone said she was getting out of the way for another baby and they were right. I was soon pregnant with my second baby, a son Willie James, just sixteen months after Ojetta's birth.

When you become a mother so many things change. You think I have these little ones to think about, to raise them to the best of your ability. You become their first teacher. You want to be the best mom ever. You hold them, teach them how to eat, to brush their teeth, then later how to make wise decisions and be good, kind, God fearing human beings.

I am a mother to many children. I had two of my own and two through marriage. I don't like the term stepmother. I also have several god children. Others I have adopted or are my spiritual children, my God children.

I love all my children as if I had given birth to them. I could never hurt them in any fashion, only love and nurture them. I love them/you all so much and God loves you more!

My "children" call me Mama, Mother and Mom. What they call me doesn't matter, whatever title they have given me as their "Mother" I am proud.

But it all began with those first three little lives the Lord entrusted in my care and who called me "Mama" – My dear son Harry, my beloved daughter Ojetta and my precious Willie James.

XII

"Cap" – My Son Harry

As I said earlier Deacon Brown had a sweet precious son named Harry. Harry was adopted when he was an infant. He had a twin named Larry who was adopted by another family – Mr. and Mrs. Moore.

Mrs. Moore's father was very close to his grandson, Larry. Sometimes he would drive by the Brown's house and the two boys would wave at one another. Each family told the boys about their brother.

Larry's Granddaddy drove by the house one day. This was the first time I had witnessed Harry and Larry smiling and waving at each other. Harry and I were in the yard. Harry asked me how they could be brothers and not living with each other.

He caught me completely off guard. I suggested we sit on the porch and I tried to explain it to him. I had a few questions including how long Harry had known he had a brother and who had told him.

Harry told me he had known for two years because his daddy and mother had told him. He hesitated in saying "his mama." I supposed he did not want to say "his mama" because he thought it would hurt my feelings.

I told him it was alright to say "his mama" because she had been his mother and been a very good mother. I told him his mother and father had loved him very much and treated him like a little prince.

I didn't want to rock the boat but here I am, not just his mother but a new mom, trying to explain to my son how this had happened, how he had a brother that lived in a different home and had a different family. I told Harry "Son, I will explain this to you the best I can."

I asked Harry if he had asked his parents why he was in one place and his brother was living at another place. He said, "Yes, Mom." I asked him what they had said. He said they had told him he was too young to understand. He said he had been asking for two years.

I began my explanation. I said "Okay, honey. Another lady birthed you and your brother and left you at the hospital. Your mom and daddy heard about it and so did Mr. and Mrs. Moore. They went to the hospital to see you both. They told me that you were such beautiful babies, smiling and looking healthy. Neither family had any children. When they saw the two of you, the Brown's chose you and the Moore's chose Larry. Both families were well established and had love they wanted to share with you boys. I think that was a good decision don't you?"

Harry asked, "But why did they split us up?" I almost cried and said, "Honey, I don't know. Maybe they thought two babies would be too much for one family at a time. Maybe the two families came at the same time and made that decision. Maybe they were each so happy and excited that they didn't think about it." Harry said "You're probably right."

I asked Harry if I had made it clearer or was it still "muddy." We both laughed. He said, "It was much clearer." Then he came to me and we hugged. I really cried then.

I was dreading telling my husband about my conversation with Harry. When Norman arrived home I told him I had something to tell him after dinner. He said he didn't want to wait, so I asked him to sit down.

I told him how Harry was concerned that he had a brother that did not live with us. I told him the explanation I had given Harry. Norman said, "You just came and you're messing things up."

I said, "Wait! Hold it! Harry is almost eight years old and he has been asking you for more than two years the same questions he asked me today! This is not my fault. It is your fault. How long were you going to wait before you tell him? He needed to hear this from you and not in the streets." I stopped talking and told Norman that he could now speak.

Norman did not want Harry to ever know he was adopted. He said he wanted Harry to think that he and his wife Margaret had been Harry's real parents.

I told him that they were Harry's real parents. The lady that left the twins at the hospital had given birth to them but they, Norman and

Margaret, were the ones that had loved him. They were the ones who had taken care of him sick or well, taught him everything he knew and that journey was continuing. I said, "You can't be more real than that!"

He said, "Sugar babe, I am sorry. It was not your place to tell him but you had to do it because I was slack on what I was supposed to do. But I tell you what, I am glad you did. I have dreaded this for so long. You did a better job explaining it to him than I could have anyway." Then we called Harry and sat down to a nice dinner.

During dinner Harry said, "Daddy, Mama explained to me about me and my brother living in different places." My husband asked Harry if he had understood. Harry said "Yes, Sir." And explained it to his father just as I had told him. Harry was in the second grade at the time. Harry seemed satisfied with the explanation and did not ask about it again.

Harry was a very manner able child. He was not sassy and did not talk back. When he was in the 7th, 8th and 9th grades he delivered the Greenwood newspaper, The Index Journal, after school. He sang in the young people's choir and often sang solos at church. He was busy with practice at church once a week.

My husband always told Harry that he should be smart like his sister Ojetta. I told him not to talk to Harry like that because each child is different. Harry had to study more and pay more attention.

Harry and Larry did not go to the same elementary school but they did attend the same school starting in the seventh grade and through high school. The other children and teachers knew they were brothers because they were identical twins. Their parents could tell them apart but other people would really get confused.

Sometime Harry and Larry would play jokes on people based on their identical looks. Their voices were also similar so they could call each other's girlfriend and pretend to be the other. They enjoyed the attention.

All through elementary, middle and high school Harry played football. He was the quarter back at Brewer High School and led the team to wins in some awesome games. He also played tuba in the band. He was busy in other activities as well

Harry would have heavy nose bleeds when he was in elementary school. I would apply ice packs to his nose to stop the bleeding. He later outgrew this problem.

Harry had this big Afro and wore flared leg pants and platform shoes that were the style when he was in high school. I would purchase his slacks and suits from this well-known men's store in town.

When Harry finished high school, Norman and I gave him a graduation party. It was a lot of fun. After the party Harry and his friends went to see the movie "Midnight Cowboy."

Harry's senior class went to Daytona Beach, Florida on a trip. He came home talking about how nice it was. I told my husband we must go there also. The next month we packed up the car and headed to Daytona Beach for nine days. We took Ojetta with us. She sat in the back seat and read. We had a long weekend before returning to work on Monday. We enjoyed the vacation.

After graduation Harry moved to Salisbury, NC to attend Livingstone College where he studied business administration and management. Livingstone College is a private, historically black, four-year college affiliated with the African Methodist Episcopal Zion Church. Harry attended Livingstone College for two years.

Harry had a friend that was going to school in Florida. He told Harry about his school and praised it to the sky. The next semester Harry was going to be a junior at Livingstone College. He talked to me and his dad about transferring to the school in Florida. We were both kind of skeptical. Harry went on and on about the school. We decided to check out the school.

The school, Florida State College, was located in Jacksonville, Florida. Florida State College was established in 1965. It is part of the Florida College System and offered a great number of four-year bachelor's degrees.

My husband and I both took off three days from work to go and check out the school. Harry was so excited. My husband told me he hoped this school was as nice as Harry had been told.

We left on a Sunday night to be there early Monday morning. Ojetta stayed with her grandmother. So that Monday we were in the school's office bright and early.

They had someone show us around the campus. It was very nice. They showed us the living quarters. The rooms were very clean and freshly painted. No alcohol or drugs were allowed on the campus. Last but not least, they took us to the financial aid office.

Everything sounded good. They were more expensive than Livingstone College.

They already had Harry's transcript from Livingstone College. We were impressed with the college. We went home and began the wait to find out if Harry would be accepted. Finally they sent us a letter stating that Harry had been accepted and he would transfer with his junior status. God is good!!

We were so happy for Harry. He was on cloud nine. He enrolled at Florida State that fall. His twin brother Larry was in North Miami. He would visit his brother on some weekends. On one of his visits he met a beautiful young lady named Virginia Oliver.

Harry and Virginia got married some years later in 1990. I always knew she was the one for him. Virginia had two adorable children from a previous marriage, Pam and Greg.

Harry and Virginia visited me for Christmas in 2010, two weeks later he had a stroke. In 2013, while still recovering from the stroke, he was diagnosed with cancer. Through it all Virginia has remained by his side. She is a wonderful wife, caregiver and daughter-in-love.

They celebrated their 25th wedding anniversary on June 8, 2015.

XIII

Lillian Ojetta

My sweet daughter Lillian Ojetta was born at Brewer Hospital on Tuesday, September 27, 1960 at approximately 10:30 AM. Dr. John Harrison was my attending doctor for her birth. Although I had my son Harry first, I was so happy to now have a daughter.

We had planned to name her Lillian Cardella. We had found the name Cardella in a baby book which said Cardella meant "bringer of light."

My mother said "if you don't name her Ojetter, I'm going to call her that anyway." My mother said Ojetter was the name of the daughter of a white lady she had worked for.

Then my mother-in-law said that name was too long. She thought Ojetta should have been named Peggy. Mother Brown had a daughter named Polly.

I said to myself the next baby's name is just for my husband and I which we did. We named our youngest son Willie James after his daddy and his uncle, his daddy's brother. But our precious baby girl was named Lillian Ojetta. I went to school with a girl named Ojetta, and I liked that spelling better.

Ojetta's wasn't the only name change in our family. My son Harry Norman dropped the Norman completely. My sister Cherry's name was Cherry Arthur Lee. My mother named her Arthur for her daddy and Lee for her mother, Leora. Cherry at one point changed her name to Sherry but I talked her into going back to Cherry.

I was in the hospital for five days because I had had a C-section. One day I heard my baby crying. I wanted to go and pick her up. In those days, they only had certain times for you to bond with your baby.

I heard one of the nurses say, "I will be glad when she takes that crying young'un home." When that nurse came in to my room I let her know I had heard what she said.

I told her she wouldn't be as glad as I would be to take my baby home. I said, "She is probably hungry and needs to be fed." It gave me so much pleasure to tell her that. She was shocked that I had heard her remarks.

I was so happy to get home with our little "pride and joy." Harry was smiling to meet his little sister.

I did not want a lot of people coming over at first. But how do you tell your friends, neighbors and family to not come see your new baby? You just pray that your baby won't catch anything from the visitors.

Later we noticed that Ojetta would cry when she had a bowel movement. We carried her to a specialist, Dr. Bell. Her rectum was too small and had to be dilated once a week until she no longer experienced any discomfort when she had a bowel movement.

Ojetta wanted you to hold her all of the time. I wanted to just sit and hold her too. I made sure she was not hungry and was dry. I would lie her down on her stomach. Now they say to lay babies on their backs. She would sometimes cry but soon go to sleep. Sometimes she would play with her little rings or bears hanging down in her playpen. She was a friendly baby, walking at eight months. She had a walker. She wanted to take off in that walker like she was running. You had to stay out of her way.

Ojetta's daddy didn't want her to cry. One day he went to visit a neighbor and she began to cry. I knew she was not hungry and she was dry so I let her cry.

By the time my husband returned home she was sound asleep but then a neighbor came by. She asked, "Irene is your baby alright? When I left to walk down to the store she was crying and when I came back she was still crying."

Norman said, "You had my baby crying?" I told him "Yes." and added, "I had to finish cooking and she is just fine."

I started to work when Ojetta was one year old. At first my neighbor, Mrs. Mattie Patterson, had a child care business and she kept Ojetta for us. Something minor happened at the daycare and my husband said I might have to stop work to take care of "his baby" myself. I told him she was "My baby" too and I would make sure that we found a good person to take care of her.

I knew my mother would take good care of her granddaughter. By that time I trusted her and Ojetta loved her grandmother. So I talked to my mother about keeping Ojetta for us while I worked.

I had to be at work at 7AM and my husband had to be at work at 8:30AM. He would take Ojetta to my mother's at 7:30AM and I would pick her up around 3:30PM. I was soon pregnant with our son Willie James. I worked until my seventh month then I took over care of Ojetta again.

After Willie James was born, my mother once again took over care of Ojetta while I recovered from the C-section. I went back to work when Willie James was six months old. I was so elated to be back at work again.

My neighbor Mrs. Patterson took care of Willie James. My mother kept Ojetta and we paid her well. My husband and I considered having Mrs. Patterson take care of both Willie James and Ojetta but we thought Ojetta would really benefit from the special attention she got from her grandmother besides by then my mother had pretty much claimed Ojetta.

Ojetta's father would pick her up from her grandmother's house. Most days Ojetta would cry to go back to her grandmother's house and her father would come home empty-handed. I would ask him "Where is my baby?" He would say "Sugar Babe, I had to take that child back to her grandmother." That's when I decided that Ojetta had to be picked up and come home every day unless it was very cold outside.

My mother didn't want to accept pay. She deserved it more than anyone else because she did a good job loving and caring for her granddaughter. She said, "That's my grandbaby. You don't have to pay me!" I am sure that she enjoyed the fact that we paid her so well.

My mother treated her grandchildren with so much love and kindness. I think she was trying to make things right by her own children with her love and affection for her grandchildren. She would go all out for them.

One day she heard my husband Norman getting on Ojetta about something. I think it was Ojetta sitting in church with her friends, talking during the service. Her daddy was telling her she was not supposed to be talking in church and to pay attention to what the speaker was saying. He told her if it happened again that her mother would put her on punishment. I said, "Oh no, Mr. Mister, you are going to put her on punishment. You saw her!"

I was in the "Young Adult Choir." We sang the first and third Sundays. The Senior Choir sang the second and fourth Sundays. After that incident Ojetta, who was about four years old at the time, always sat with me.

If it was a Sunday that I had to sing, I would ask a friend if Ojetta could sit with her. After my mother started to come to church with us, Ojetta would sit with her grandmother.

When my mother heard Norman say he was going to punish Ojetta if she talked in church again she got so upset with him. I asked my mother why she was so upset about this. Ojetta was taught not to talk in church. Her father was chastising her firmly but with love.

Growing up Ojetta liked to attend church and Sunday school. Ojetta loved to talk about her careers when she grew up. There were three things she said she wanted to do as an adult – science teacher, lawyer and movie star.

One day over dinner, I said, "Darling, you are making me tired thinking about all the things you are going to do when you grow up." She was so intelligent and learned easily.

Her father gave her the nickname "Grandma" because she was wise for her age. I did not call her "Grandma." Her brother started calling her "Jett." I called her Ojetta sometimes, but most times I called her sweetie, darling or honey bunch. All the sweet names I could think of.

Ojetta went to a private kindergarten at four and five years old. At age six she entered first grade. She was so smart they moved her to the second grade. She enjoyed going to school but there was one teacher that was prejudiced. We moved her to another school after a meeting with the teacher, principal and school board. She always did great in school. Ojetta enjoyed studying and always had her head in a book.

The new school was much farther away from our home but it was worth it. Her daddy took her to school every day. We had a carpool that brought her home in the afternoon.

Ojetta's father, Norman Brown, died when she was twelve years old. She was in the seventh grade. I remarried when she was about to turn fifteen and going into the tenth grade. We moved to Calhoun Falls, SC where my husband David Edmunds had his home.

Ojetta was depressed as she was still grieving not just her father, but her aunt Cherry and her grandmother who had recently died. She was also sad that she had to leave her friends and the city she had grown up in. She had been looking forward to attending Greenwood High School.

Calhoun Falls was a much smaller city. Ojetta felt that this was a good move for me and I felt that it was a good move for her. We were each putting on a brave face for the other. Ojetta did make friends in Calhoun Falls. She got her driver's license at age fifteen.

Ojetta was promoted to the twelfth grade the following year and graduated with honors from Calhoun Falls High School at the age of sixteen. She was voted "Most Talented" in her class. At age sixteen she was ready to head off to college.

When my daughter Ojetta was sixteen years old she was invited to go for a ride with a guy she considered a friend. He came in for a minute when they returned and then she walked him back outside. I went to the door to look out and see what they were doing. I saw a quick kiss. I was recuperating from surgery so I went back in the house to lie down.

After he had left Ojetta came into my room and sat down. She looked disgusted. She told me that had been a terrible kiss. I said "You didn't like the kiss?" She said "Ugh! No Ma'am." The way she described the kiss, as if it was the most disgusting thing ever, I asked her nonchalantly if she liked girls. She said "Yes."

I was not expecting that answer! I was already on sick leave. Had I not been, I am sure I would have had to take some time off. I was so devastated. Maybe I had been in denial but I cannot recall thinking that she might like girls before this night. I just stayed in bed and cried. At that time my eyes were not as dry as they are now so I could shed tears.

Later Ojetta asked me something that shocked me. She asked if I would love her any less. Through my tears I said "NO!"

How could I love my daughter any less? I said to myself "Lord this is hard!" I wondered how I would survive this. I also knew it would be hard for her. I thought what I did wrong to make her this way.

This was in May. I could not talk to anyone about this not even David Edmunds, my second husband, who I was married to at that time. One day he said to me that someone had asked him if Ojetta was gay. Ojetta and I both denied it. I was too ashamed. Ojetta thought her step father would be ashamed of her too and look down on her. It was a very hard time for me and her. Finally I told my husband about it. He said "Oh, hell no!"

Ojetta and David Edmunds had several conversations after that about her being gay. Despite his initial reaction, after their talks he came to accept it.

As I said I did not have any support so I turned to prayer. I prayed "Lord I need your strength for myself and my daughter." Remember this is my story and I am telling it as it happened – the good, the bad and the ugly.

Ojetta met another young man. They both knew the other was gay and became the best of friends, confiding in each other and spending a lot of time together. He was gay but pretended to others that he wasn't. When Ojetta returned home from college one weekend everybody was asking her if she and the young man were engaged as he had been telling everyone. (He wanted Ojetta to cover for him). Ojetta didn't lie, she said, "Engaged!?! No Way!! That's my brother!" Even though they had been the best of friends, that young man refused to speak to Ojetta from THAT day to this. She was heartbroken because she really felt that he was a dear friend. I can't imagine how hard that must have been. Oh yes I can, of course I can, I went through it myself and I saw my daughter go through it. People saying they love you and pretending to be your friend; while all the time thinking, they are above you, talking behind your back and laughing about you. Not easy at all, to say the least.

Gays and lesbians need all the support you can give them, even when you have family members that are turning their noses up at you. I have seen later on some of these same family members later come out of the closet as gay also. Some come out later because they knew they were not going to be accepted gracefully.

I am glad Ojetta did not wait to acknowledge her sexual orientation. I know now that it really took a lot of courage. I just had to deal with it and let her know she was loved unconditionally by me if no one else. I did not understand it!

I told the Lord you made her in your own image, if this is wrong, now you can change her. I told him I cannot change her. "You are her creator.

You have to do the changing. All I can do is pray one day she will change. I can and I will go on loving her."

I could not even say my daughter was gay. Again, I say it was difficult! As time went on she met some nice, intelligent, educated ladies. I would think why not some intelligent, educated handsome men. I would pray "Okay in the spirit and in English. I wanted to hear from the Holy Spirit about my daughter. I knew the Holy Spirit would tell me the truth.

I knew what I had read in the Bible. What others have said and continue to say. But this day I asked the Holy Spirit to speak to me, his prophet, and answer some questions for me.

I told the Holy Spirit that women being with women seemed to be so nasty, The Holy Spirit replied "No nastier than women being with men."

I said "But they cannot procreate." The Holy Spirit said "There are enough children in the world without another child being born." The Holy Spirit told me other things too!

I do not lie on any one. I certainly would not lie on the Holy Spirit. I thank the Holy Spirit for telling me the truth about something I have long struggled with. I want you parents, sisters, brothers, grandparents, uncles, aunts, cousins and friends to seek the Holy Spirit for your answer.

Twenty-five years later, I feel so much clearer and informed about the subject now. We need true information and education. I do feel that I can teach others on this subject. You know, actually, the Holy Spirit said I could truly teach others on this. The Holy Spirit always teaches the truth. He could not lie. He cannot lie because there is only truth in him. When he spoke to me I knew that I could rely on his word. Hallelujah!

Lying in bed thinking about what the Holy Spirit said to me about my daughter being gay, I heard him say "You didn't mention the other thing I said." I said "No, I do not want to bring that into this book." The Holy Spirit asked "Why not? Tell the whole story!" I said "I will catch flack for what I have written already."

The Holy Spirit said "You wrote what I told you to write. Now write it. Some of my disciples were gay. The readers must understand you are not saying this, I, THE HOLY SPIRIT SAID IT!"

I said "Lord, I don't want any of my readers to confront me. I will not debate anyone about this at all." The Holy Spirit said "If they have questions, tell them to ask me!" I said "Thank you Holy Spirit!"

Now I feel free to say that my daughter is gay and if you out there don't approve, it is between you and the Holy Spirit. I am so grateful for clarity in Jesus holy name. You must remember this information came directly from the Holy Spirit – his words not mine! I was in shock myself but I knew I would get the truth.

Don't be ashamed of who you are. You and I could have been born this way. If I had been born gay I would appreciate having the love and support I have given to my own daughter. I have other family members and friends that are gay. I did not expect the answer I received from the Holy Spirit.

The Holy Spirit reminded me "You remember saying to me that if this is wrong, I want you to change my daughter. You noticed I did not change her because in my sight it is not wrong. I am the one that matters. My ways are as different from your ways as the east is from the west. I am proud you are no longer worried or fearful about your daughter being in good stead with me."

Ojetta graduated from South Carolina State University with a Bachelor of Science in Psychology in 1981. She was employed at the Department of Social Services (DSS) as a social worker in Abbeville, SC. She enjoyed working there. I had people walking up to me on the street telling me how nice my daughter was to them and how they appreciated her going the "extra mile" to help them. I felt very proud of her as a mother.

Ojetta moved to Michigan in 1985. She began working as a counselor within weeks of arriving in Detroit. She returned to school and received her MSW from Wayne State University in Occupational Psychology and Mental Health. She has been a counselor and an advocate for many different groups of people from newborn to 100+ yrs. of age. Helping them to improve emotional issues, relationship, family and health problems. She has been blessed to work as a Clinical Social Worker, Psychotherapist, and the staff clinical psychologist in Clinics and Hospitals in Michigan. And the best part is, she loves what she does!

In 2000 my daughter Ojetta was ordained in the ministry of the Assembly of Justified Believers at New Covenant Church in Detroit. She knew she had a calling as young as six years old. She spoke to ministers at other Churches before her ordination. They would take her under their tutelage but would have a problem when they realized she was a lesbian.

I wanted to attend her ordination but my husband, Alfred Washington (my third husband) was going to have surgery so I could not. Ojetta seemed to understand. I know in reality that she wanted her mama with her on that special day and I wanted to be there.

I can always depend on her to keep her word. I thank the Lord she did understand the position I was in. She always thought about "Daddy Washington" too, not just about me. I love her for that. She has a heart of gold!!!

In 2001 Ojetta married Connie Piper. Connie was and is a lovely lady. When Ojetta had a closed head injury in 2003, Connie took excellent care of her. I was unable to travel due to my husband Alfred Washington having surgery. I called her often to check on her but I really wasn't worried about her. I was concerned but I knew she was in good hands.

Connie was a very kind and loving caregiver. I know it was not easy for Connie because of the seriousness of Ojetta's injuries. Thank God after five years of rehabilitation and extensive therapy Ojetta has regained most of her previous abilities.

Ojetta and Connie were married for seven years, but unfortunately it did not last. They remain the best of friends. It's amazing to me that they are now just like sisters. Connie remains like a daughter to me and I am like a mother to her.

I am happy to say that my daughter has at last met the love of her life in Michelle Brown. When my daughter talks to me about Michelle, it reminds me so much of the relationship Alfred Washington and I had – genuine joy and love, no bickering or arguing, always pleasant and understanding. They light up when they see each other. I always wanted that kind of love for my children.

Ojetta is now the Chief Executive Officer (CEO) and founder of her own business, the Center for Peace Counseling and Holistic Healing. It is amazing to watch your child grow into the woman she was born to be… strong, intelligent, loving, God-fearing and more.

I call Ojetta my sunshine but I know it is the Light of God shining through her. I could not be more proud of her than I am and thankful to have been the vessel that God chose to be her mother.

On March 17, 2015 I was cooking breakfast and the Holy Spirit said to me, "If heterosexuals don't stop judging gays, it is going to be more gays in heaven than heterosexuals." All I could say was, "WOW!" and I wrote The Holy Spirit's words in my journal.

XIV

Willie James

Ojetta knew what she was up to when she started walking early. She was getting out of the way for her baby brother, Willie James.

I discovered I was pregnant shortly after I returned to work when Ojetta was about one year old. I worked through my seventh month of pregnancy. Willie James was born by C-section.

I began to feel strange right after Willie James' birth. I could feel life going out of my body, going down from head to about my waist. I could see my husband, my son Harry and daughter Ojetta.

I couldn't speak, all I could do was think. I thought to myself, "Lord, do not take me from my family and life." I began to feel life come back into my body. The nurse came in to give me a shot. I heard her tell someone that my skin was like rubber. Dr. Harrison came in the room. I told him I almost died, He said, "I know."

Both Harry and Ojetta were happy to have their new baby brother. He brought so much joy to our family.

He was thirteen months old when he died, a darling child. He died from spinal meningitis. Meningitis is a term used to describe an inflammation of the membranes that surround the brain or the spinal cord.

Willie James became sick one day. He was warm to the touch and not very active. Meningitis causes fever and lethargy but these symptoms are often hard to detect in young children.

I called in to work early that morning to tell them I would be staying home with my sick child. By then he was warmer and not getting any better. I called

Dr. J. Harrison at home. He told me he was going to do rounds at the hospital in about an hour and would stop by our home to check in on Willie James.

He came by the house and prescribed medicine for the fever and pain. He thought Willie James might have the flu. On his way home, Dr. Harrison checked on Willie James again. He said, "Irene, if your son is not better by tomorrow, I will admit him to the hospital." Dr. Harrison had delivered both of my children.

I called him the next day and told him Willie James was no better. He said, "Bring him on to the hospital." That morning he came to see Willie James. By that time, a pediatrician had checked my son.

He and Dr. Harrison had a conference. They both came to me and explained how sick Willie James was. They told me there was nothing they could do to make him better.

I could not believe my ears. I took my son in my arms, held him and just cried. I think Willie James was in the hospital approximately two weeks. Sometimes he would seem to get better and then there would be another crisis

I stayed at the hospital while my mother took care of our daughter Ojetta. My husband Norman took care of our son Harry.

One morning I called my husband to tell him that our son was better. He was so pleased to hear the news and I was glad to report it. I went back into the room and the nurse was checking on Willie James. He began to roll his eyes up and down. The next thing we knew, he was gone.

They tried to get me out of the room but I was not leaving. I cried and cried. I thought now I have to call his daddy and reverse the good news I had just given him. I dreaded making that call.

When I finally called him, Norman came to the hospital immediately. I fell into my husband's arms. He began to cry too. I thought "We have just lost our baby son."

I do not remember the ride home. I do remember our oldest son Harry was cooking bacon – mostly burning it – and he was sobbing. I went to him and embraced him. I said "Son, I know how you feel. Let me finish this." Actually, I cut the stove off and he and I sat down.

My husband was outside talking to neighbors. One of my son's friends came over. I got up and began cleaning. One of my neighbors, Mrs. Spearman, came over. She said, "Everything is clean. It must be your nerves." I said, "It must be." I had cried out for the time being.

Most of our neighbors – Hazel, Mary, Eloise and Janie – were at work but came to our home when they got off. Mrs. Spearman was retired. Mrs. Patterson came over. She ran the day care and had kept Willie James for us while we worked. Mrs. Yeldell came and prayed for us. Bessie got off from work and came to check in on me. So did Mrs. Anderson who prayed before she left. Mrs. Anderson cooked breakfast for us. I don't know if anybody ate or not.

Ojetta was still with my mother. She was about three years old at the time of Willie Jame's death. He died on Monday morning and we had his funeral on Wednesday. My neighbors, friends, family and church family were all so kind to us. I did not go back to work for a month.

During Willie James illness I became aware that I wanted to become a nurse. The staff at Brewer Hospital had been so wonderful to us. I thought if I could impact some one's life the way the nursing staff had impacted my family during that difficult time I could really be of service.

I would pick my son up from Mrs. Patterson as soon as I got off duty. After his death, I felt strange not picking him up after work each day. My arms felt empty for a while even though Willie James had started walking at eleven months.

After Willie James died I really wanted another baby but I had had a tubal ligation after his birth. I wish I had waited. Back then doctors said you could have three C-Sections, I had had two. Maybe people need to wait and be sure this is what they want unless there are health issues. I did not have a health problem. I thought three children were enough. – Three made our family complete.

I talked to my husband about adoption. He said, "No." so I said, "Okay". I do believe we made the right decision about the tubal ligation because I was so sick after Willie James was born. I had a near death experience.

I think now about this Bible verse, "Now unto him who is able to do far more exceedingly abundantly far more than we can ask or think, according to the power at work within us...." (Ephesians 3:20). I couldn't ask but I could think. Glory to God!! Thank you Jesus for the thinking!

That is when my husband and I decided we were not going to have any more children and to thank God for the children we already had. Some couples are not as blessed as we were.

XV

Life with Norman

The church ladies weren't the only ones after Deacon Brown.

My mother told me that women could easily take my husband because I talked about how I wanted my husband to treat my girlfriends if they came to visit. If they needed a ride home, I wouldn't mind if he gave them a ride home. I wanted him to be polite and a gentleman. Mother said, "Oh no! You're making it easy for him to be unfaithful."

Norman had been involved with a Caucasian woman named Ann. His wife Margaret had been ill a long time and he had needed companionship. He and Ann had gone out twice. He had gone to her house once. He had been afraid someone would drive by and see his car at her house. He was so nervous that he couldn't go there again. He had explained to Ann that being married and a deacon he had to repent and ask for God's forgiveness. He said Ann kept after him hoping to rekindle the relationship.

Norman's relationship with Ann had resolved before Margaret died. After Margaret died, she thought she had a chance but the prospect of an interracial relationship was just too stressful for him. He again told her there was no hope for them.

She would call the house and not even acknowledge me. She would just say "Let me speak to Norman." I would just hand him the phone.

After a while I asked him what was going on. He denied everything. She was the secretary where Norman worked.

One day Norman and I went to the office to sign some papers. The secretary, Ann, was acting so strange. She was trying to be nice to me but was finding it very hard to do so. Norman was prancing around in the office with his hat in his hand. He kept twirling the hat round and round.

I thought "Is it possible they are having an affair?" If so, is it over, is it on going, what? If we saw her out someplace you could tell she was not happy to see us together.

One day I said to him, "Listen. I know something is going on with you and this lady." He said I was wrong but I knew I wasn't. I always heard where there is smoke, there is fire. There was a lot of smoke, so it had to be a big fire.

One day when I came home after I got off duty from the hospital I found Norman in bed not feeling well. He pretended he was sick because I had charged too much at a department store. I told him I hadn't spent much and I was paying for it. I asked him why he was so upset about this bill.

He finally got up and said, "Honey, you know the bill is not that much. I know you like nice things and I want you to look lovely when you dress up to go out." He said he would pay the bill.

I still could not understand why he was taking it so hard even after agreeing it wasn't too much and saying he would pay it. Why had a bill sent him to his bed and why was one of our male neighbors sitting with him.

When the neighbor left he finally got up from bed. I asked him what was going on. Then he told me Ann had killed herself. I said "Oh no!" and asked him what had happened. He said he thought she had taken an overdose of pills. Then he began to tell me about their relationship.

After we married Ann was highly upset. She felt he was rejecting her because he now had a young wife. Norman told her that he did not want to see her and it had nothing to do with the fact that he had a young wife. His first wife was young too. He told her that they should never have gotten involved with each other. It was a mistake and God had forgiven him for that.

She was an attractive lady. I believe she loved him and on some level he may have loved her too. But he was not willing to go through being a Black man in the South married to a white woman.

I wish he had told me earlier about this situation, maybe I could have assisted in some way. I maybe could have understood somewhat or at least, if I had some of this information, I could have prayed for him and Miss Ann.

I can imagine how hard it was for her. Norman did have me and Harry but she was all alone. I could tell that my husband was truly sad. I tried to comfort him the best I could. Never once did I judge him. He was judging himself hard enough. So I tried to lift him up spiritually.

This was not the only secret from Norman's past. He also revealed he had a daughter from another relationship early while he was married to Mrs. Brown. I asked him where this daughter was and why she was not living with us. He said the child was living with her grandmother in Greenwood, SC near us. Her mother lived in Asheville, NC. I had known his daughter Shirley Ann for years, never knowing she was my husband's daughter. So many secrets. I believe his drinking helped him cope with the guilt he was carrying.

When we first got married he drank too much. I would talk to him about his drinking, that it was not good for our marriage or our family. At one point it had gotten so bad that I was about to fall out of love with him. I loved Norman Brown but this was about to fade. I did not want this to happen.

We talked about his drinking over and over again. I knew that he did not want a divorce, neither did I. I wanted my husband and my children needed their father. Finally he said "Sugar Babe, I am putting the alcohol down because you and these children mean more to me than anything."

It did not take him long to get rid of that alcohol addiction. I was so elated and thankful the day he told me alcohol no longer ruled his life. He did it! I know the Lord had to help him. My God can do anything if you believe he can in Jesus name!

I prayed and asked the Lord to return my love for my husband as strong as it was in the beginning. The Lord heard my prayers and restored it even stronger than it was at first in our marriage. With God all things are possible to them who believe. We were a happy family again!

Norman was tall with a dark complexion, handsome, friendly and kind once the alcohol was removed. He loved his family. He loved to surprise me with clothes, furniture, diamonds and even a new car once.

We had our ups and downs, more in the beginning while we were adjusting to each other. After about a year or so things just started to fall in place. I was deeply committed to my husband and family. There were temptations but nothing and no one could shake my love and commitment to them although some tried.

My mother told me that women could easily take my husband. Mother said, "Oh no! You're making it easy for him to be unfaithful."

I believe when people have it in their heart to do right, they will do it. On the other hand, if your heart is not right, male or female, they will do wrong. When you genuinely love a person, you will treat them the way you want to be treated. Love is not supposed to hurt, to make you feel pain. If it does, something is dreadfully wrong!

Check it out! The mind set of "I do you wrong/you do me right" won't work. It won't work in friendship, in courtship, in marriage, in a work relationship or in any other kind of a relationship you are trying to have.

I was working at the Greenwood Shirt Company. We were on production when I first started. It was so hard. You had a very fast sewing machine. Fortunately I never stitched my hand as some of my co-workers did.

I was a shoulder joiner. My job was to attach each shoulder to the shirt. The supervisor would bring each seamstress a bundle. The bundle contained 200 pieces that needed to be sewn together. You were supposed to sew the number one to number one and the number two to number two and so on. when I first started, being new to the job, I would sew the number one piece to the number 100 piece and the number two piece to the number 99 piece which was incorrect.

I had such a nice supervisor. Her name was Mrs. Ashley. She would take apart the pieces I had sewn incorrectly for me. I would start over. Fortunately, I caught on quickly and was soon, doing it right. She was so sweet. I soon was able to make production by 12 Noon and start on the next day's work. You didn't really make any money until you got production which was your quota for the day. You were paid more for anything over production.

I did shoulder joining. The next group did the collars. I enjoyed that until the machines would break and put you behind on your production. Sometimes the mechanics would be so slow.

There was a certain mechanic, who was Caucasian, that routinely fixed my sewing machine. I asked him one day, "Why are you the only one who fixes my machine?" He said it was because he liked me. I asked him when that happened – his liking me. He said since you first came here to work.

I told him I was happily married and asked him if he was married. He said yes. I said apparently you aren't happily married. He said, "Yes, I am!" I asked him if he loved his wife. He said yes. I told him tonight tell your wife you love her, better yet show her. After that conversation, he did not fix my machine unless he was the only one available.

One day he said to me, "Brown, that talk we had worked!" I told him to keep it up. His mind set had changed. He only needed the reminder to have it in his heart to do right in his relationship and their relationship was rewarded.

I knew then I wanted to be a counselor. I find myself giving advice that helped people. Sometimes they just want you to listen and to not judge them.

I hear people say, "I can do bad by myself!" I say "I don't want to do bad, by myself or with anyone else either. I don't want to do bad, period." I hear the Word of the Lord say, "My God shall supply all our needs according to his riches in glory by Jesus Christ."

When I think back on the situation with that mechanic I realize it could have gone either way. I asked him if he was so happy in his marriage, what had happened that caused him to be displeased. He said he liked to party on the weekends and to flirt on the weekends. I told him to take his wife to the parties. I asked him when he flirted did he ever take it to the next level. He asked me why.

I told him because I could have gone to the next level with him but I had chosen not to. He said that sometimes he did take it to the next level. I told him to treat his wife the way he wanted to be treated.. When you genuinely love a person, you will treat them the way you want to be treated. That is My motto!

He asked if my husband knew how lucky he was. I said I believed he knew how blessed he was. He and I believed in the same motto.

We weathered the good times and bad, with love.

XVI

Death of Norman

After the accident that took the life of my beloved sister, my first husband Willie "Norman" Brown, the father of my children, became ill. He was hospitalized November 28 and died on December 1, 1972 just three months after Cherry's accident.

On that Thursday, November 27, 1972 I called him from work to say hello. I didn't usually call him from work but I knew he would be home as he came each day at noon for lunch.

He told me he had my Christmas present. I asked him, "Why did you get it so early?" He said, "I saw it and wanted you to have it!" I thought that was strange. I thanked him for being so thoughtful.

When he came home around 5:30PM he had my presents. He had two presents wrapped so pretty. He wanted me to open them. I didn't want to, but I did it for him.

I opened the big one first. It was an AM-FM radio shaped like a can opener. It was very unique. The smaller package was a beautiful, approximately one karat, diamond ring.

He also had gifts for our children Ojetta and Harry. For Ojetta he had a tape recorder. It was wrapped beautifully. He advised her to continue her music studies. She had a beautiful voice as did her brother Harry. He had a card for Harry who was away in his junior year at college; as a matter of fact, he had cards for Ojetta and me besides our gifts. There was a check in each card.

I was so happy. I drove over to show my mother. By this time our relationship had been mended and I enjoyed sharing these things with her.

My mother loved my presents and asked if Norman would purchase a radio for her. She said she would pay him for it the next day. When I returned home, I told Norman what mother had said. He said, "I'm going to go get it right now." I told him it could wait until the next day but he insisted on getting it immediately while the radios were in good supply. I said, "But honey it is 6:00 PM. They close at 7:00PM and you will be there in the morning at 8:30 AM so there will be plenty left." But I could not get him to wait.

I felt so strange getting our gifts a month before Christmas, even stranger opening them right after Thanksgiving. I could feel in my spirit something was about to happen. That night he had a stroke. My husband had tried to warn me prior to this but I did not want to accept it.

I called Dr. John Harrison and told him to meet us at the emergency room as my husband had had a stroke. He asked me if I was sure. I told him I was. I had already called 911 and asked Dr. Harrison to please hurry.

He met us at the E.R and confirmed Norman had had a stroke. We were both concerned about Norman's heart also. He was admitted there and then. Ironically he was admitted to room 584 on the floor I usually worked on, in a room I had actually discharged a patient from earlier that same day. I was a certified nursing assistant then and was taking classes at Tri County Technical School.

The hospital provided a bed for me to sleep on so I could stay by his side and assist in his care. I would get up through the night and suction him so that he would not choke on his saliva. It was hard to see him so sick. I stayed with Norman day and night. It was a trying time, just losing my precious sister after her tragic automobile accident. She and her family had all been patients at this hospital. The staff, my coworkers were so supportive.

When Norman was hospitalized, I called his daughter Shirley Ann's grandmother and her aunt and told them about her daddy's condition. Shirley Ann came to the hospital. She said she felt like my husband Norman was her father. I asked her, "Isn't he your daddy?" She said, "Yes, but I didn't know if you knew." I told her that her daddy had told me everything. I was glad she came. I told her that her dad could hear her.

Hearing is the last of our senses to leave. When I wanted to say something that I did not want him to hear I would go into an empty room next door. I would go there to pray and make my calls telling family and friends how sick he was.

Cherry's husband, my brother-in-law Norman Thompson Sr. came and spent the night and helped shave my husband. My husband was too sick to get in the shower. An orderly had to help me bathe him in the bed. This meant a great deal as my brother-in-law had not been long discharged from the hospital himself following the accident that had taken Cherry's life. I went and spent the night with my mother. I still remember her snoring and the woodpecker outside the window pecking. I did not get much rest.

I got up at 5:00 AM and went back to the hospital about 6:00 AM. My brother-in-law said Norman had rested all night. When I looked at my husband I realized his condition had worsened. I noticed that he wasn't as alert. His breathing was shallow and his complexion had changed. My heart just sank. He died that day around noon.

I called the school to have Ojetta sent home. She was in the 7th grade. My friend Bessie Baylor went to pick her up. Ojetta came in the hospital room and looked at me. I looked at her not knowing what to do. We stared at each other then I put my arms around her and just hugged her. Then I made the call to my son Harry summoning him home from school.

Before long my friend Sister Bessie Baylor came back over. She had lost her husband about six months before Norman died. I spent a lot of time comforting her. Now she was doing the same for me. Other friends and family came to see me.

My mother had been taking care of Ojetta while I had been at the hospital with Norman. I knew Ojetta was in good care. My mother treated her grandchildren with so much love and kindness.

I could not believe what was happening to our family. The deaths of my Norman and Cherry were so close and we had all been so very close to each other.

When I was a small child I use to hear my grandmother say, "When it rains, it pours." I would look outside and the sun would be shining. I thought what is wrong with my grandma - it's not raining. I now know what she meant.

Ojetta began to talk about dying. It broke my heart. Our oldest son Harry Norman Brown took it very hard also. Norman died the first of

December and Harry returned to college the beginning of January the next year.

I suppose it was about two months before my husband died that he told me he wanted me to know how and what bills he paid each month including the house note and insurance, etc. I told him that would not be necessary but he insisted that I needed to know. He told me where the insurance policies were. I told him I did not want to hear this.

I told my mother what he was doing and she told me I needed to listen to him. I said I would listen but I didn't want to hear it. Mother said, "Mrs. Brown your husband knows what he is doing." I believe he knew he was getting ready to leave me and our family.

I told Dr. Harrison after Norman died, I wished Norman could have lived even if he was in a wheelchair. Dr. Harrison said I was selfish. He said as active as Norman was he wouldn't have wanted to live that way.

I had not thought about it like that. I wanted Norman here on earth with me and our children. The more I thought about what Dr. Harrison said I realized he was right but that did not lessen my pain.

I prayed day and night for strength. My husband told me before he died that he wanted me to marry again. I thought I didn't know anyone I could even date much less marry. Norman said the Lord would send me some one. I thought to myself "I don't think so!"

I gave Norman a beautiful "Home Going." Lots of people at the church from Greenville, SC, Georgia, New York, Illinois, North and South Carolina attended. The people blessed us with so many flowers and so much food. Our son kept saying, "Mama everything is going to be alright." The senior choir sang my husband's two favorite hymns – "What a Friend We Have in Jesus" and "Amazing Grace." Rev. Ed Johnson was our pastor. He asked the choir to sing these songs every month for a year.

I kept thinking at the funeral how I had wanted him to live, prayed for him to live and yet he had died. I did not understand it then. I just wanted Norman to be alive and to be there with me and our children. I know now there are worse things than death.

Rev. Ed Johnson did a beautiful eulogy. He talked about when he first came to Morris Chapel after the retirement of Rev. H.B. Mitchell. Norman was his deacon, smiling while the others were frowning. Norman did have a pleasant smile. When he saw a lady he would always tip his hat and smile.

Someone asked me how do you like your husband doing that? I told them he does the same thing when we are together that he does when he's alone. I had accepted that this was just who Norman Brown was.

My husband was friendly to everyone male and female. Some Sundays when I was at work, Norman, Harry and Ojetta would go to Sunday school and church. When I came home one Sunday Ojetta said "Tell her daddy! Go on and tell her!" I said tell me what?

Norman said "Sugar babe, Mrs. So-and-so hugged and kissed me and Grandma (his nickname for Ojetta) didn't like it. She said would you like it if Mama hugged and kissed a man?" Ojetta was about five years old. He told her "Grandma you're right!"

Yes, we had our ups and downs. If you were to ask me would I marry Norman Brown again, knowing all I know now? My answer would be, "Yes I would!" He put me and my children before himself. I put him and our children before myself. Everyone was taken care of with the highest esteem.

My mother, baby brother Joe and I

My sister Cherry age 14

XVII

Widowed, Single Parent and Family Responsibilities

After Norman's death I had this hole in my heart. I was about to the point that I did not want to get close to anyone, afraid they were going to die and leave me. But I had to keep myself together as much as possible because I had Ojetta and Harry. They needed my continued love and care.

My son Harry was in college at the time. Ojetta was twelve when her daddy died. I was a widow at age 32 caring for my children and helping with Cherry's children, Chip and Ivey.

I started to talk to this gentleman that lived on the next street from us. He was handsome, intelligent, light skinned but not real light. He had a beautiful smile and was tall and slim. He was a nice kind man. He was divorced with two daughters and two sons.

I talked about Norman; the things we did; and the places we went. I did not know anything else to talk about. I apologized for our whole conversation being about my first husband. He told me he fully understood. He could tell Norman and I had loved each other. I asked him how he knew. He said because every time he had seen us we had seemed so happy. I told him we were, that we could make each other laugh. He said that is how you tell.

He said sometime I would pass his house on my way home from work. I would wave and speak. He said he thought to himself that seems like a nice lady. Our conversations went on and on like this.

I was working at the hospital. I went to Tri-County College to take more courses in the nursing field in the evening for another 18 months and obtained an associate's degree in nursing (ADN) then passed the national licensing exam. I was able to manage financially because Norman had planned well for our future. There was insurance to pay the house off in the event of his death so we were able to continue living in our home in Greenwood, SC. Norman also left me his pension and had excellent life insurance.

When I finished school, I became employed at the DHEC (Department of Health and Environmental Control) in Abbeville, SC. It was a nice place to work. I enjoyed going to work each day. I worked from 8:30 AM-5:00 PM with an hour for lunch unless we had clinic days and then only 30 minutes. Other days we had outreach which were home visits. I was responsible for getting charts ready for and assisting the doctor at the clinic and following up with patients.

Days at the hospital were different. You worked hard but it was rewarding. I worked there most Sundays. I didn't work Sundays at DHEC. I had so many days off including Memorial Day, Veterans Day, Presidents Day, New Years, 4th of July, Thanksgiving, Christmas Day and sometimes Christmas Eve. I am sure I have left some days off. We had sick leave and vacation days. I met a lot of wonderful people at both places.

Ojetta was between 12 and 14 years old. I made her breakfast and she was picked up to go to school at 7:45. I had to be to work at 8:30 AM. When I worked at the hospital she and I would get home about the same time. When I went to work at DHEC she would go to my mother's house or Mrs. Patterson's house. I brought dinner home every night, I occasionally cooked.

Ojetta functioned well at school, she got excellent grades however she was still depressed. We were both depressed but we really didn't know how to talk about what we were feeling. My daughter had pretty much shut down her emotions and would just come home, lie on the sofa and watch tv. She did not feel like doing anything and I understood that because that is how I felt too. How I wished I could have lied on the sofa and be out of it also but I had too much to do.

I often drove around like a zombie. I really didn't know how to help my child, I was on automatic pilot. I told her I loved her and gave her a lot of hugs. I encouraged her to do the best she could and told her that I knew how she felt. I prayed for her all the time, I didn't know what else to do.

Harry was depressed too. He put on a brave face and tried to reassure me that everything would be all right. Looking back he must have been in a lot of pain with the rest of us. He returned to school. He had financial aid to cover most of the expenses and he worked. I helped him financially also.

XVIII

Reconciliation and Caring for Mother

I always had to help take care of my mother mainly because of her poor vision. It was a labor of love even as a child despite my mother's abuse. She was my mother and I loved her even when she could not show me the love a child expects from their parent.

I am forever thankful that God touched her and changed her heart. My care for my mother did not end when I got married. I had a family to take care of and that family included my mother.

After I married Norman we heard about an ophthalmologist in Greenville, SC who was supposed to be very experienced in eye surgery. I made an appointment for my mother and drove her to Greenville to have a check-up by this physician. He checked her and took x-rays. We were to go back in a week. When we went back he said that he did not think surgery would help her. My mother was so disappointed. I was too.

For the next two weeks I could tell my mother was disappointed. After the third week, I called to get an appointment with the doctor to have a consultation with him. I asked him to please do the surgery on my mother's eye. I told him that at that point she couldn't see anyway so there wouldn't be anything for her to lose. I told him she believed the surgery would help her. I begged him to please do the surgery on my mother's eyes. Finally he agreed. I was so happy. My mother just cried and thanked me, again and again. They did the surgery two weeks later.

My mother stayed in the hospital for almost two weeks. I drove her back twice to remove the bandages and twice for check-ups. My mother could see not totally but her vision was restored about 75%. She could safely walk to town by herself. She could see her children and other people as well.

One day I went by her house after church she told me my dress was too short. She asked my husband, "Norman don't you think Irene's dress is too short?"

He said, "Mother Oglesby, I think the length is alright so long as I am with her." My mother laughed.

Another Sunday we went by after church. I had long beautiful hair that my mother had not wanted me to ever cut; but that Friday, I had gotten it cut. I had forgotten that mother could see now. She had been blind for so long. When I came in the house she looked at my short hair and asked my husband, "Norman, why did you let Irene get her hair cut?" He said, "Mother Oglesby, I was not happy, but she wanted it cut and it does look nice!" He told her I had received many compliments on my hair at church. I reminded my mother that my hair grew fast and it would grow back. She said, "Oh, so you have cut it before?" I had to confess, "Yes ma'am."

I was so happy my mother could see. She could dress herself and cared about how she looked. She even started wearing makeup again. During her recuperation I cooked dinner for her, my sister and Pop Lewis every day after getting off work at the hospital. It was quite a task.

About three months later my mother-in-law, Mrs. Brown had to have eye surgery. We called her Mother B. I drove her to the same ophthalmologist in Greenville where she had surgery. I now had another person to cook for – Mother B. and my mother.

When I cooked I made enough for my family, my mother and sister, and my mother-in-law and brother-in-law who lived with Mother B. It was not easy but God gave me the strength to work, pick up my baby Ojetta and cook for everyone.

My husband wanted dinner ready at 5:30PM. If it was almost cooked by that time he was fine. He told me if I could not have dinner prepared on time he would rather I not work.

I enjoyed working so I had dinner on the table at 5:30 PM, no later than 5:45 PM. I had approximately two hours to get everything ready. Most days it was ready at 5:30 PM very few times, it was a bit later. He did not complain. After having to cook for more people, Norman had no time limit on dinner.

I cooked from scratch every day. My mother cooked for us a lot before she had surgery and even more often after she had surgery. After my son Willie James died she cooked while I was going through a period of depression. We all were depressed then, even my mother and mother-in-law.

My mother mostly cared for Ojetta while my husband and I worked. Our neighbor, Mrs. Patterson, took care of Willie James. Mrs. Patterson grieved a lot for Willie James after his death also. I think my mother was able to mourn better than I could because my husband and son didn't want to see me cry. I held my tears the best I could even though that was not always in my best interest.

I have cried more writing my story than I have in many years. Over the years I have developed "dry eye syndrome" which also has made it hard for me to cry. Sometimes I cry through my nose. I told my doctor about this. He said a few people do this when their eyes are very dry. When I do shed a few tears, my eyes get irritated, burn, itch and feel gritty. Before my eyes became dry I was able to cry without a problem. I do need to take some time and grieve for all my loved ones that have passed.

In June, 1973, my mother was diagnosed with uterine cancer. I resigned my position at the Department of Health and Environmental Control in SC to take care of her.

My supervisor Miss Beatrice Courtney was Director of Nursing at DHEC. She wanted me to take a leave of absence instead of retiring. I told her that I didn't know how long my mother would need me and I knew that during this time they would need to have someone in that position.

When my mother met my father she told him she did not want children. My mother told me after they got married and she got pregnant with me she tried to abort me, She said she tried everything, took all kinds of strong medicine. She said she would even hit her stomach with her fists. She tried not eating to starve me to death but that didn't work. She said the more she tried to abort me the more I grew. She thought I might be deformed at birth, due to all she tried to do before my birth.

If God is for you, man can not harm you! My mother told me so many times she didn't know what she would do without me. She said, "You have been so good to me. Well or sick, you were always there. I could depend on you. You were there physically, emotionally, spiritually and financially." I told her, "Mother I am happy to be here for you."

Mother grieved so terribly hard after Cherry's death, she was ailing physically and emotionally. She became really ill in May 1973 which was just five months after Norman's death. I paid Ms. Angeline Rogers to stay with her during the day while I worked and on the nights that I had class. Pop Lewis was there to take care of her and sometimes Uncle Stead would come to help with her care.

When my mother became ill I wanted her to come to my home and stay but she wanted to stay at her home. It wasn't too bad as we stayed about seven minutes away from each other but the reality was I now had two homes to take care of.

Mother was cold in the summer while I was hot. I had air at my home but she only had fans. When it got too hot, the fans did not help. By the grace of God, I kept trusting him to help me and my mother. God is our refuge and strength, a very present help in time of trouble (Psalms 46:1).

Ojetta was still shut down emotionally from Cherry and her father's death. She loved her grandmother so much and could not talk about her grandmother's illness and the possibility of her dying too. When she visited her grandmother she would try to put on a brave face when in her presence. Afterwards she would go in the other room to cry and pray. I could not have my child going through that, I didn't insist that she go visit her grandmother often. Harry came to visit her but didn't stay long. It seemed that it was important for him to appear macho and to put on a brave face as well.

My mother died October 5, 1974 on a Saturday afternoon at approximately 5:00 PM. My mother died from uterine cancer when she was 54, so young and vibrant. I thought when I was 54 I was going to die too. On my 55th birthday, my daughter Ojetta said, "Mama you made it!" Yes, praise the Lord – I made it in Jesus name!! Through it all God is good.

After my mother's death Miss Courtney asked me to return to my position at DHEC. After my resignation they had hired another person but by the time of mother's death, she had gone to Viet Nam with her husband. The position was open. Miss Courtney said I could come back, not as a new hire but, with the same seniority I had had when I left. I had stayed off of work for four months after my mother's death. She already had a list of clients for me, had called headquarters and arranged for me to be reinstated with all privileges.

It is hard to write about my sister's accident and death and harder to write about my mother's abusiveness. My daughter Ojetta said, "Mama tell the whole truth. It will help someone else do the same."

XIX

David Edmunds

I met Mr. David Edmunds, Sr. from Calhoun Falls, SC before my mother's death.

One day I was out in the community as a nurse visiting patients in their home. I was looking for one of my patient's home, according to the directions I had been given.

I must have driven pass the address. I saw a house being built and thought that would be a good place to turn around. As I was turning around I backed into the mailbox. A gentleman came up behind me. I thought he must know I was lost and was going to help me. I don't know why I thought that, but that was the first thing that came to my mind.

He pulled up to the side of my car and I asked him if he knew my patient. He said he thought she lived on the street to the left. Then he blurted out, "You knocked down my mailbox. That's a federal offense!"

My knees started to shake. I thought "I can't get arrested, Lord!" I thought about my mother who had just been diagnosed with uterine cancer, my own children, and my sister's motherless children. I had paid a lady to take care of my mother while I worked. I couldn't go to jail!

He told me to follow him back to the mailbox. It was laying in the ditch. When I had turned around I had heard something hit the car. I had gotten out of my car and looked at the fender. It was not dented and I remembered the mailbox as still standing. There were four mailboxes and apparently I had knocked one down. I told him I was sorry for the damage and asked what I owed him.

He wanted to know who I was and where I was from. I introduced myself. He told me he was David Edmunds Sr. I asked him again what I owed him for the mailbox. He told me to forget about it.

I said, "You got into your car, followed me down the street and now you're saying I don't owe anything." I was getting angry, which I seldom do. He said, "Give me a dollar". I said, "A dollar? Here take this five dollars. What are you going to do with a dollar?"

He told me he was building the house I had seen and wanted me to come and look at it. I asked him if he thought his wife would appreciate some other woman looking at her house. He told me he was in the process of getting a divorce. He then asked me what my husband would think about my looking at his house. I told him that my husband had been deceased for three years.

The fact that he told me that he was in the process of getting a divorce instead of saying that he <u>WAS </u>already divorced made it seem that he could be an honest man. I felt comfortable talking to him. Also, in the south people tend to be more friendly and open. I told him about my mother's illness.

It turned out one of his sisters-in-law was a very good friend of mine. We also went to the same beautician. Mr. Edmunds asked her if she knew me. She asked him if he was talking about Deacon Brown's widow. He said he didn't know all of that. She told him if the woman he was talking about was Deacon Brown's widow, she is a nice lady.

So we talked for a while. My mother was not getting any better. I think I was in denial. I was thinking, hoping and praying for her to get better but she was only getting worse.

As time went by a friendship ensued. I told him that I did not have time to date as I was taking care of my ailing mother. He said he didn't want me to neglect my mother. He said he would come and help me take care of her.

I couldn't trust anyone to take care of my mother the way I could. People were telling me to put my mother in a home but I told them, "No way!" As long as the Lord gave me health and strength I was determined to care for her myself. I knew she couldn't be loved and cared for the way I would.

Mr. Edmunds understood and told me he did not want me to neglect my mother. He said he would help me. I thought this was truly wonderful because I could surely use the help. My sister had been killed. My brother Joe was living a wild life at that time. (Joe has, since that time, given his life to Christ and is a deacon in his church.)

My brother-in-law, Cherry's husband, came to help some but he was still recuperating from the accident. I was more or less on my own.

David Edmunds was true to his word and faithful in assisting me. He would help me with her bath. He would even run errands for me.

He would come and cook – he was a very good cook. My mother, at one point, would tell me what she had a taste for, I would cook it but she could not eat it. She would then tell me something else she had a taste for but she couldn't eat that either.

I would take her to the hospital to get treatments three times a week. When I brought her home she would be so sick. How my heart went out to her. I had to pray for her strength and mine.

By this time mother was so sick she could not get up to the bedside commode. She had to wear adult diapers. I had to roll her from side to side.

She didn't like using the bedside commode when she was more able. When it became hard for her to go to the bathroom I asked her if she would please use it. She did it for me. I thanked her and told her how much I appreciated it.

Mr. Edmunds came every morning between 10 and 10:30 AM. I would have given her breakfast most mornings. Mr. Edmunds and I had a routine. After breakfast he would help me with her bath, bed change and combed her hair. All that took from 2-4 hours.

He would start dinner while I finished up with mother, Sometimes I would have to go shopping before he could cook depending on what my mother had a taste for – sometimes beef roast, potatoes, carrots and cabbage. After one of us prepared the meal I would fix her plate and hoped she would want it. Sometimes she would just want a hot dog and I would fix it. Other days it would be grits, eggs and applesauce. I never knew what she would have a taste for or if she would eat it.

Sometimes my legs would be swollen from lack of rest. Edmunds would say go lie down on the sofa while he stayed to watch over mother. He would usually leave each day between 5 and 6:30 PM. He was so much help to me. How I thanked God for Edmunds assistance. This continued for over a year.

One day he told me his divorce was final. I was not happy to hear this, I would rather that marriage had lasted. Early into the second year of caring for mother, Edmunds asked me about marrying him or our living together. I told him I wouldn't live with him without marriage and I didn't know how I felt about marriage at that time. I didn't know how long my mother would need me. After her, my children were my first priority. I didn't know how that would work with a marriage. I had a lot to pray and think about.

My Uncle Stead came from Edgefield, SC the Tuesday before her death. On Wednesday night, mother was not doing well. I asked him if he thought I should call my brother Joe to come home. He said he thought I should. I called him that Wednesday and he came early on Friday. My Aunt Mary and some of the family came from Augusta, GA that Friday night before mother died. So Saturday morning everyone was there. I had to order groceries. I asked everyone what they wanted and if they wanted something special. I made a list and went to Winn-Dixie to shop.

Edmunds and Pop Lewis, my mother's former boyfriend, and my brother brought the groceries into the house. Edmunds and my Aunt Mary cooked. I was up talking and entertaining everyone. Edmunds said, "Lillian you need to be resting while you can." I thought about it and went into the living room and laid down on the sofa. It was about 3:45 PM

Edmunds came and woke me up. He said Aunt Mary said my mother was not breathing. I was just waking up and asked what he meant my mother was not breathing. I asked him to go check on mother. When he returned he said she was breathing.

By then I was fully awake. I went up to check on her and she was gone. My mother died that October 5th on a Saturday at approximately 5:30 PM.

My Aunt Mary and I along with others began to cry. I called the doctor who came right over and pronounced her dead.

I called Parks Funeral Home which was just two houses up the street. They came and got her body. I knew my job there was finished. I told the family and friends that were at my mother's house, that I was going home.

Some people did not like that I chose to return to my own home after my mother's death. It was so hot at mother's house.

From June 1, 1973 to Oct 5, 1974, I was at my mother's house. My priority had been to take care of my mother and, if I do say so myself, I did a good job! I gave my mother the best care there was and I thank God for that. So I felt that my job was complete and I was at liberty to go home to take care of my baby Ojetta. Even though she was fourteen years old, she was still my baby.

Even family members were upset when I left my mother's house to go home. I was privileged to have been there as long as my mother had needed me even with the heat and all. But after her demise she no longer needed me at that house.

I went home. My daughter Ojetta was lying on the sofa. The house was nice and cool. My son Harry was in Miami, FL with his brother Larry for the weekend. Harry came home for mother's funeral.

Near the end, when mother was really deteriorating, Ojetta spent the nights with her friend Marcella Strong. Marcella's mother was my friend. They knew to go to Marcella's way before dark. I would call and check on Ojetta to make sure she was doing alright. David would stay with mother while I took Ojetta food every day.

Ojetta loved her Grandma but could not bear the stressful environment or the extreme heat at my mother's house.

The night of mother's death, I got home before dark. Neighbors began to come to the house. The family received some mourners at my mother's house. I also received them at my house.

Mother's funeral was the following Thursday at 2:00 PM. Dr. Ed. Johnson did a beautiful eulogy. One of mother's favorite hymns was "Sweet Hour of Prayer." I had Sarah Butler and Bessie Baylor in the family section as my sisters. My friend Julia Mae Hill Holiday from Manning, SC came and spent the night before the funeral. She cooked breakfast the next morning for everyone.

XX

Marriage The Second Time: David Edmunds

After Mother's death, David Edmunds asked me to marry him. I told him I would, after Ojetta went to college.

He would come over and go to church with Ojetta and me. Sometimes Ojetta and I would drive to Calhoun Falls and go to church with him. Sometimes he would cook dinner on Sundays for the three of us. Other Sundays I would prepare dinner for us.

Mr. Edmunds wore some good looking shoes. I think I fell in love with his shoes. But seriously, after he was so faithful to help me with my mother, I thought he would make me a wonderful husband and be a wonderful father figure for Ojetta. Over this period of two years I began to love Mr. Edmunds.

Edmunds and I married on Saturday August 9, 1975 at my home. Pastor Henderson Louden performed the ceremony. Ojetta was my maid of honor. We had refreshments at the reception at Bankers Trust Hospitality room. It was full of family, friends and guests. My best friend Julia was in charge of the bride's book. Edmund had too much alcohol at the reception and tried to hit on her. I thought "What have I gotten myself into?"

We moved to Calhoun Falls, SC when Ojetta was fifteen years old. David Edmunds had a big five acre farm. It was a big deal to us, moving to the country. He had a big tractor that plowed up the sweet potatoes. Ojetta and I would go out in the field and pick them up. Neither one of us were excited about picking up the sweet potatoes. I knew he had worked so hard in the fields. One day I told Ojetta "if my friends back in Greenwood could see me now!"

Our home in Calhoun Falls consisted of four acres. David had a tractor and plowed one acre for his vegetable garden. In addition to sweet potatoes, He also grew green beans, crowder peas, squash, cabbage, turnips, collards, okra, and tomatoes. He sold all of these vegetables to neighbors.

One Saturday morning, he had an errand to run and told me that if anyone came by and wanted to buy some turnip greens there was a certain price he wanted per pound. I told him that was too much. He said, "That's all right, just wait till I get back, I'll handle it.'" But when people stopped by to purchase something, I would put an extra pound or two in their bag.

I started a small garden on the other side of the house that had radishes eggplant, carrots, celery and beets. I wanted to do root vegetables. Root vegetables can be very intimidating. Most of them have thick strange looking skin and long stems with leaves sprouting out of them. Ojetta said that they looked like they were from outer space. We spent many hours shelling peas and in other ways preparing the vegetables to cook or freeze. Though Ojetta wanted nothing to do with the farm life, she had to admit, when prepared properly these vegetables were absolutely delicious.

David Edmunds was a heavy drinker when we married. I thought when we married he would change. If only he would stop I thought things would be fine. So we went about our married life, going to church, having dinners for friends and family. I loved to cook and entertain.

Looking back now, I realize that my marriage was an attempt to fill a void, but that never really works because you haven't taken the time to heal.

I went to work every day. David Edmunds was a good father to Ojetta, even though it was obvious that he was not accustomed to being affectionate. Ojetta was accustomed to getting hugs but he would kind of pat her on the back. She somehow understood that he was doing the best he could.

David would instruct her on how to do things around the house that she did not have to do in Greenwood like cutting firewood and bringing it inside. He was patient most of the time. David considered himself an expert on everything so he and Ojetta would get into some lively debates. They enjoyed each other's company. He was an excellent cook and conversationalist. There was no jealousy or rivalry between the two of them.

Ojetta went to South Carolina State University at age sixteen. I missed her so much. We were very close and talked often. One month the phone bill was $400.

Ojetta and David got along well. He had two children with his first wife – David Jr. and Cheryl. David Jr. was in law school and Cheryl was teaching at the time of our marriage. I had met his first wife soon after our marriage. She and their children were nice and respectful to me. In fact she and I became the best of friends. The family called her "Bea" but I called her "Betty." We were both Christians and it was easy. She was an elegant sophisticated and dignified lady.

I enjoyed when his children David and Cheryl came to visit also. Cheryl was married at the time of our marriage. David Jr. married after he graduated from college. As they started their families we all, David Sr., Betty and I, enjoyed and shared these grand children with no conflict.

Edmunds and I traveled a great deal. I would say yes before he could finish asking if I wanted to go someplace new. Ojetta traveled with us before she went to college and when she was home during the summer. We visited most of our relatives and friends across the United States and Canada. Some of the most memorable trips were to the beaches of Florida and South Carolina, and the cities of Washington DC, Harrisburg PA, Philadelphia PA, Chicago ILL, Baltimore MD, Detroit MI, Buffalo NY, Niagara Falls, Birmingham AL, as well as Augusta and Savannah Georgia.

David Edmunds and I did not have sweet pet names for each other. Sometimes I would call him babe but he always continued to call me Lillian. I felt that I loved him more than he loved me.

His drinking continued to get worse. One day I told my daughter Ojetta that I was thinking about getting a divorce. She reminded me that alcoholism was a disease. She said "You wouldn't divorce him if he had cancer, would you?" I said of course not. So I continued to pray for him to stop drinking. Ojetta knew that David flirted but thought it never went any further than flirting.

One day after I had returned to work as a nurse, I was out home visiting. When I arrived back at the office I could barely get out of the car because of pain in my back. The clerk and Director wanted to take me home but I knew I needed to go to the doctor. I could not drive so they took me to the doctor and called my husband, David Edmunds.

David came and had his brother with him who drove my car back to Calhoun Falls. David stayed with me at the doctor's office. X-rays did not show anything but a little arthritis. They diagnosed a pulled muscle and gave me pain meds and muscle relaxers.

I was out of work for three days. I went back to work the following Monday feeling better. I saw a few patients that came in to the office and did some paperwork. Periodically I would get up and walk around to ease the continued pain in my back

Ojetta was in college at South Carolina State University. My husband had dinner prepared each day unless he was busy doing something else then I would pick up dinner on the way home. One night he had cooked fresh corn, steamed okra and sliced tomatoes from our garden with fried chicken and lemon aide. I don't think anyone likes good fried chicken like I did. They say all preachers love fried chicken. The food was so good.

David said "Lillian, don't make yourself sick. I don't want to have to call Tippy (his brother Robert) to take you to the hospital." His brother worked with the EMS. I knew I had eaten enough of his delicious food.

I was still having a problem with my back. My aunt Mary told me how her back had been a problem for her. I didn't think my aunt's back pain could be that bad, actually it was worse than that. Now I was experiencing back pain. It was worse than anything I had imagined. I didn't understand what she had been going through, so I really hadn't empathized with her properly. Now I did! We really need to be careful how we judge other people when they are talking about their pain. Because if you have not experienced something you are really not in any position to comment.

She said she wanted me to go to her doctors and made an appointment for me to see an orthopedist, rheumatologist and a neurosurgeon. They checked me out. They x-rayed my back and came to the same diagnosis –spinal stenosis, degeneration of discs, osteoarthritis, and slipped disc – recommending bed rest, pain meds, muscle relaxers and a back brace.

Spinal stenosis is a narrowing of the open spaces within your spine which can put pressure on your spinal cord and the nerves that travel through the spine through to your arms and legs. It causes pain tingling numbness muscle weakness and problems with the normal bladder or bowel function. Spinal stenosis is most commonly caused by wear and tear changes in the spine related to osteoarthritis (when the protective cartilage of your bones wear down) in severe cases of spinal stenosis doctors may recommend surgery to create additional space for the spinal cord or nerves.

This treatment went on for a while. The neurosurgeon Dr. Estes told me that although he made money doing surgery on backs, he would not touch my back with a ten foot pole unless I was paralyzed. He predicted that I would be in a wheelchair within a year.

That was over thirty years ago. I say "Greater is he that is in me, than he that is in the world!" I give God praise for still walking and standing, in Jesus name.

I was told to come back in a year for reevaluation. I went back ten months later. My back was the same no further degeneration. At that time they did an orthoscopic of my right knee also. It had gotten to the point when I stood to walk I would almost fall down. In fact, I did fall down a couple of times. The knee problem was due to osteoarthritis. They did arthroscopic surgery on the knee and l had physical therapy. A year later I had Lasix surgery on my right eye.

Six months later my husband David went to the VA hospital to have a hernia operation. He had a heart attack during the surgery. It was quite a lengthy recuperation. At that time he stopped drinking and smoking – seven years after our marriage. I was so sorry about his heart attack but was elated that it had prompted him to stop smoking and drinking. It was one of those situations that you call bittersweet. During his recovery I developed shingles which was quite painful.

So many friends, church members and family were by my side. Especially my brother Bishop Emanuel Spearman and my second cousin Deacon Willie David (WD) Butler. They both came while my husband was in the V.A. Hospital in Augusta, GA. My brother came as often as possible although he was very busy with revivals, funerals and other pastoral duties. Cousin WD came to visit us every week.

WD was more like a brother than a cousin. We were very close. He had three names that he called me: Ms. Rene, Cuz Rene and Daughter.

He told me "Daughter if you need me just let me know." Then he said "David I am as near as your telephone. I will be here next week but if you need me before then I will be here." That meant so much to both of us. Every week we could depend on him sometimes after church, sometimes on Sunday. Some Sundays WD would have dinner with us.

My dear cousin WD died April 18, 2014. I had planned to fly down to visit him on April 22, 2014 and had scheduled my flight but the Holy Spirit said I needed to go a week earlier. My daughter Ojetta changed my flight to April 15th.

When my first cousin Jean Simpkins called me and told me about WD's passing I was in total shock. I had planned to visit him the next week. I told my daughter Ivey, who I was staying with, during my visit, and her family. My granddaughter Ebony mourned the loss of WD whom she called her "slow eating" cousin. I called my daughter Ojetta in Michigan. They all knew how close I had been with WD. We were all so very sad.

I arrived on Tuesday and he passed the following Friday. The home going services were the Monday before the day I had initially planned to arrive, therefore I would not have been present for the funeral. But praise God for the Holy Spirit leading and guiding me, I made it there in time.

My sweet brother Bishop Spearman picked me up for WD's funeral. My darling daughter Shirley Ann went with us. I did not have a hat with me so my brother went and purchased a fancy black hat for me. He knew my style!!

Back to those days following David's surgery in 1982. My cousins Louella and George Washington came down from Greenville. Louella had cooked all this food and brought it with them. They stayed several days. George and David went to Sunday school and church while Louella stayed with me. I was so glad they came to visit us. They are such dear cousins and friends. They left that Sunday evening. A few years after this Cousin Louella died. I went up to help Cousin George to assist with her before she died. David and I went to Greenville the night before the funeral.

I got sick that night with pain in my left side. I had this throughout the night. The next morning my cousin fixed breakfast. My husband and I went to George and Louella's home before the funeral. I was getting sicker. I told David I needed to leave and go to my doctor in Calhoun Falls.

David could tell I was getting sicker and sicker, so he stopped at the emergency room at Anderson Memorial Hospital in Anderson, SC. They asked me when I had had a heart attack. I said "A heart Attack?" I did not know I had had a heart attack. So they admitted me to the hospital. They did a heart cauterization and found out that I had 30% blockage. I was in the hospital for a week.

I had orders from the doctor to take it easy for two weeks then to return for a checkup. Things were better at that checkup and I returned to work two weeks later. Everyone was so nice to me, remembering me with cards, flowers and visits. My pastor and his wife put me on their prayer list.

Mr. Edmunds started to drink again and not a little, too much. I did not like the drinking. He did not seem to be able to control it.

He told me he was on medications. I asked him what kind of medications. He showed it to me. I looked it up and found it was a pain medication. He was not supposed to be drinking with this medication. The potency with the alcohol had kept his symptoms hidden from me for a while. He also smoked. I did not like smoking or drinking. Mr. Edmunds was also a womanizer. At first I thought he was only flirting but when I found out for sure there was more than just flirting involved, that's when I knew it was time for me to leave. The situation was causing me to be sick and I was visiting the doctor every other day.

David Edmunds and I separated on May 5 1992. I initiated the separation. I moved in with my daughter Shirley Ann. I just called and told her that I had left David. She was sad that I was hurt but happy that I had made the decision to remove myself from a situation where I was not happy. We were divorced September 13, 1993. I was very hurt over it. I had hoped the separation would have opened his eyes. I finally told him we couldn't seem to make the marriage work. I had hoped we could remain cordial with each other.

Once he told me we shouldn't have ever gotten married. He said he felt sorry for me. I never really figured out what that meant. Looking back at it now, I guess he saw that I had been through so much tragedy that he thought that he could add some joy to my life even if he wasn't prepared to really make any changes in how he approached the commitment of marriage.

I don't think he thought about the heartache his behavior would cause. Even at our ages when we married, we were both still immature in many ways. I learned so much about myself by being married to David Edmunds.

I would not rush into a relationship with another man. I would have to heal and hear from God if I were ever to be married again.

I never talked against him before or after the divorce. Sometimes people get along better after the divorce.

Edmunds is a good person with many good traits but he is not a man who should be married. I must admit we did have some great times together. Every one that knew him would tell you he was a big time flirt with a kind heart.

Betty Edmunds, David's first wife, and I remained friends. She was very understanding and emotionally supportive. His children and I are on a cordial basis and talk from time to time.

After all these years, David Edmunds and I remain on a friendly basis. He is concerned about me and I am concerned about him. We talk on the phone about two times a month and even now, Ojetta and I make a point to visit him whenever we are in SC.

Unfortunately, just before the publishing of this book, Mr. Edmunds died on January 27, 2016, peacefully, at the age of 95. I am so thankful that he had accepted Christ approximately 6 years before his passing. He will always be remembered fondly by me and my family.

Single Again: Life Goes On

After the divorce my daughter Ojetta came from Michigan to be supportive. She invited me to live with her in Michigan. Harry was married and living in Florida. Staying with him was not an option. I had never wanted to live with any of my children – Harry, Ojetta, Shirley Ann or Ivey.

Living with others is so different than living on your own. Some people change a lot, some just a little and some not as much. Most of my friends were very supportive and understanding. My aunt Mary was quite disapproving. She and David's sister Fannie, thought I should have stayed with him and dealt with the situation. They didn't understand doing so would have been too stressful for me.

When the divorce was final I found a place in Edgefield, SC the place where I was born and where many of my cousins lived. I decided to get my own place. I wanted to live alone and do things for myself. I had all of my things from before my marriage to David Edmunds in storage to set up my new home. I had retired and had only my retirement income to live on as I was not receiving any alimony support from David Edmunds.

I began to walk early each morning. I would be walking around 7AM or earlier. I walked for about an hour, I began to lose weight and feel really good. After ridding myself of all the stress related to my marriage and starting to walk regularly, I felt better all the way around.

Even David Edmunds commented on how nice I looked. I could not believe he said that. I thanked him. He asked me if one day I was coming back to him.

I asked him if he had changed. His reply was that he liked his life just as it was. I said I wasn't coming back to the same old thing.

During the last years of my marriage to David Edmunds, my self-esteem was low. I felt like a failure. I had done all I knew to make my marriage work and yet it still failed.

I was unable to make my husband value the things I valued and to understand the importance of sobriety and fidelity. He never changed. At the end of our marriage he was the same person he had always been intelligent, adventurous, flirtatious and unwilling to really settle into a monogamous relationship.

You can't change anybody but yourself! I initially felt that all of those years had been wasted; that I had been a fool to expect a drastic change when he didn't want to change. I was broken. When our marriage ended I had to pray harder than I had ever prayed before for strength and for direction.

It was hard. I cried a lot. I leaned on the strong arms of God, my children, my church family and my friends. Slowly, I began to do the things that made me happy. I ate better and started walking. I visited the sick and shut in and focused on helping others, encouraging them to not stay stuck in a bad situation.

Everybody was telling me that I was looking better. I was feeling better about myself. By the time the divorce was finalized, my self-esteem was great!!

XXII

Third Time's the Charm Mr. Washington

After a while, about three months, I met a nice Christian gentleman, Brother Alfred Washington. I had known him for over thirty years. I always had called him Brother Washington. He was George Washington's uncle, the people that had adopted me years ago. His niece, Margaret, was my first husband's wife. Brother Washington was Margaret's uncle. She was his brother's, Harrison Washington's, daughter, George and Margaret were first cousins.

After Margaret died and Norman and I were married, they adopted me as their cousin in her place. That was George and Luella Washington of Greenville, SC – a beautiful family. Their daughter Betty and I became good friends.

Before Ojetta was born, she came and spent her vacation with us. After Ojetta was born I had some swelling and Betty came to help. She was a lot of help. I can never forget such a grand gesture.

Once when Betty had surgery I went to stay with her for two weeks. After the two weeks I had planned to go home. I was praying one night for the Lord to send someone to help her. The Holy Spirit said to me "What do you have to do?" I said "Not anything really."

The next morning I told Betty what the Holy Spirit had said. She was so happy and I was happy to continue to assist her. God is good!!

I think I stayed three more weeks. She was much stronger when I left. Thank you Jesus for directing my path. I felt she was able to take care of herself. She was so thankful and so was her father and the rest of her family. The Lord had blessed me with such a beautiful family.

I did not believe in divorce but unfortunately it had happened to me. I thought I would have to live the rest of my days as a divorced person.

One day I was talking to the Lord about my situation. He said to me that I did not have to remain single and He would send the right person to me.

I had been to visit my friends George and Luella Washington in Greenville, SC. Alfred (Bro. Washington) was George's uncle. While I was there George said he had not heard from Alfred and his family.

When I left Greenville that night and arrived at the place where I was staying with Rev. Rufus and Minister Georgia East, (Sister East wanted me to come and rest my nerves for a while), I realized I had left a pair of glasses.

I thought about what George had said about not having seen Alfred/Bro. Washington for a while. The next week I called Brother Washington and asked him if he would like to drive to Greenville with me to retrieve my glasses. He said he could ride with me Sunday after church. I told him I would pick him up on Sunday.

I did not tell George that Brother Washington was coming with me. He was so surprised to see him. We got back to his home in Abbeville about 7PM that night.

On the drive back Brother Washington told me he had a girlfriend but had not seen her in three months. I asked him why they hadn't seen each other. He said his girlfriend had been sick and was living with her daughter who did not think her mother needed a boyfriend. I asked him what his girlfriend had to say about it. He said she agreed with her daughter because she was living in her daughter's home.

He asked me if I had a friend. I told him I was recently divorced after a year's separation. I told him I wasn't interested in dating just then. I told him that I believed one day the Lord would send me a Christian man who loved God with his entire being. He would be saved sanctified and Holy Ghost filled.

Three months later he called and asked me if I would escort him to his Christmas dinner in McCormick, SC. I didn't have any plans so I accepted. When we arrived at the dinner he introduced me as "his lady".

I thought, "I'm his friend not his lady." I enjoyed the event. Everyone was very nice to me.

After the dinner Brother Washington and I talked on the phone from time to time. He told me about his late wife and his children. His wife had passed away thirteen years earlier. He and his wife had ten children. I knew most of them. I thought his large family was wonderful.

For Christmas he invited me to one of his daughters' home for dinner. The food was so delicious. All of his children, grandchildren and great grandchildren were there. I thought it was great to see the whole family together. I asked him if all of his daughters could cook like that. He said that not only his daughters but his sons were also good cooks. He said he and his wife had taught them. I was amazed to hear about the sons cooking.

I told him I didn't believe he could cook and asked him what he could cook. He told me mac and cheese, fried chicken, corn bread and cabbage.

After the holidays I left Abbeville and returned to Greenville to stay with George and Louella. Louella was sick so I helped her with the house work and cooking. I also read to her. I stayed two weeks and really enjoyed my time there.

When I arrived home in Abbeville, Brother Washington and I went to Augusta, GA to visit my Aunt Mary and Cousin Dorothy. I introduced him as Brother Washington. Aunt Mary always had dinner for us. She was a very good cook. When we left he asked why I always introduced him as Brother Washington. I said that it was what I always called him.

About April of the next year he asked me to be his "special Friend" (i.e. dating him exclusively). I told him I needed to pray on it. I also told him that, even though he had not seen her in a year, he needed to communicate with his girlfriend to make sure they both had a good understanding of their situation.

A few days later he told me he had spoken with his girlfriend. She was not going to return to her home and agreed with her daughter, that as long as she was living with her daughter she didn't need a boyfriend.

He had told her that he had asked me to be his "special Friend" but I would not date him as long as they were together. I asked him what he and his girlfriend had decided. He said they did not decide anything.

I suggested to him that they should talk again and get things straightened out between them. The next week he went back to talk again. After that visit he said she told him that she was no longer having a boyfriend. He told her that there was another woman (me) that he had asked to be his special friend but I was not going to date him as long as they were together.

Bro. Washington said his girlfriend told him she believed that he and I were already together. He told her that was not true but if I accepted his "special Friendship" then it would be true and that he would be dating someone new. I told Bro. Washington that he should not have said that to her. It was ugly, not nice. One day I met this woman in the grocery store. We spoke a few words to one another but nothing about Washington.

He asked me if I had made a decision. Another gentleman had also asked me to be his girlfriend. I told him it was not up to me but the Holy Spirit. One day the Holy Spirit said "Brother Washington is the one for you. He is your assignment." A week later I told Brother Washington I would be his "special friend."

He was happy. I felt relieved to obey the Holy Spirit. The other gentleman was a pastor and thought we should be together. He thought because he was a pastor and I was an evangelist we would be good together. I told him I was not doing the thinking on this. I had asked the Holy Spirit. He asked me if I was sure. I told him the Holy Spirit had given me specific instructions. I was sure of my choice. And I would no longer be talking to him.

About a year and a half from the time we met, six months after becoming his special friend, Brother Washington asked me to be his wife. I had to pray again. I had reservations about getting married again. I had made out a list of the various qualities I wanted in a husband and Washington did not meet all of the qualifications that I thought I needed. But by that time I was in love with him.

The Holy Spirit told me "He is your husband. He is the one for you! As I told you in the beginning, he is your assignment." I asked the Holy Spirit what exactly did that mean – my assignment. The Holy Spirit told me "It is a task that has been given to you from me to assist him any way you possibly can."

Brother. Washington told me that he wanted to start going to school. He wanted to get more proficient at reading and writing. He had already talked to the officials, a woman at the school. I said, "For real!?!"

The teachers were husband and wife. He told me that some days it would be the wife and other days her husband. He would be going two days a week. I was in shock. I had no idea he was thinking about going to school. I asked him how he knew about this school. He told me he had asked around and someone had told him about it. He went to school every week and would bring his lessons for me to look at. I would help him with his homework. It was a lot of fun. He found learning easy.

After he had been going to school for a month I went to visit my daughter in Michigan for a month. On the way back home the bus had an accident on highway 40 West in Asheville, NC. My knee, jaw and shoulder were severely injured. I had to go to a special dentist and, of course, a physical therapist.

I had dizziness and terrible headaches. I was at home maybe a month when one morning I woke up so dizzy I fell and sprung both of my hands. My friend Irene Gordon took me to the family physician. The doctor wrapped both of my hands which limited what I was able to do a great deal.

I had talked to Bro. Washington. He said he would come and stay with me and help me. I had been talking to my neighbor. Ms. Brown was a sweet lady but she was 84 and had arthritis in her knees. My steps were hard for her to climb. Some days she would come and bring me food or send it by her son.

One day while I was talking to my daughter Ojetta, I asked her to help me pray that the Lord would send me someone to help me. Ojetta said "Mama, the Lord has sent Mr. Washington to help you. Stop thinking about what other people think. You need the help." Ojetta knew that I was concerned that the neighbors might say that Washington and I were sleeping together.

My Neighbor also said I should let Mr. Washington come and help me. She went on to say that our neighbors have their husbands and their own lives. She advised me to stop thinking about the neighbors and think about my need.

I called Bro. Washington and told him I really needed his assistance. We had not married yet so I told him that he would have to sleep in the other room. He laughed and asked me if my bed wasn't big enough for both of us. I told him "Oh no, it is not!" He began to say "I know. I will be there to be your hands and to take you to therapy three times a week – Monday, Wednesday and Friday."

Sometime my cousin Jean would bring me dinner. Most of the time Mr. Washington would go to Denny's, a real nice home style restaurant with good food. One day my cousin Dorothy and her husband, Deacon Brown, came from Augusta, GA. They had been to the store and picked up some food. They cooked a big dinner. All these wonderful cooks. We were blessed. How good God was to us.

Bro. Washington stayed two weeks, going to his part time job at West Carolina Telephone Company two times a week. On Tuesdays and Thursdays, he did a little light cleaning and stocked the office supplies there.

Then he would visit his family and friends in Abbeville on those days. He would leave Edgefield around 6:30AM to start work at 8AM. He did not like to rush and liked to be there by 7:30AM. I did not like for him to rush either.

I think during this time I began to start loving him. He was so kind, sweet and respectful. He went to church in Abbeville every Sunday and board meetings every Saturday. I told him he needed to rest on the days we were not going to therapy or when he had other activities. We would sit and talk. He asked me again about marriage before he came back to stay for another three weeks.

He said "I don't think you want to marry me!" I told him the Holy Spirit had told me he was my husband. He was surprised and said "He did? So when are we going to get married?" I told him he needed to talk to his children. He said he hadn't told them who they should marry. I told him that he was their daddy and most of them did not know me.

He said "I know you and I have been knowing you since you were married to Norman Brown. You have always been a nice lady." I told him when George and Luella had adopted me into their family, I thought the whole Washington family had adopted me. He said" I tell you, I did not adopt you!' He asked me, "What about your children?' I told him my children would not be a problem. I had already spoken to them about him.

"They want me to be treated well. My children know I will treat you the way I want to be treated (that's my motto!) They want me to be happy."

He said he thought his children would accept me. I told him that whatever he did for his children, to continue. I did not want anything that he owned. I told him "I just want you to love me. I love you and want us to be happy together." I told him I was so glad he was a Christian. Christians can get along. A family that prays together, stays together.

I learned quickly that some of his children did not take the news well. He said some of his children had come right out and said "Daddy you don't need to be getting married," while the others' disposition was cool and distant.

I thought maybe I had been the same way when my daddy and step mom married; however, I was glad for my dad because my mother was so mean to him. My daddy needed some peace in his life and some love and joy! Plus my father had married Eula Lagroom the woman he had dated when he met my mother. My mother and Eula had dated my daddy at the same time. He married my mother first and later my step-mom. I realized he was happy in his second marriage.

Mr. Washington's wife had died thirteen years before we started to date. We married five years after my divorce. So his wife was deceased approximately eighteen years before we married. I did not break them up or come between them in any way, shape or form. It is a blessing when your conscious is clear. Glory to God!

Washington and I did not consider the age difference at all. We did not talk about it because we did not think about it. I was 53 and he was 78 when we started dating. My husband was strong as a man in his healthy 40's. He told me one day "You didn't know I was so strong, did you?" He could walk miles and not get tired. I told him he had taken great care of himself.

He was 5'10" tall with dark brown skin, solidly built and strong. He stood erect, no slouching, and he moved purposefully and energetically. His hair was gray which he later shaved bald. He was a handsome man.

He told me that he was not perfect. He acknowledged that he had made some mistakes in his life but he had repented and asked God to forgive him. I told him we all had made mistakes. Since he had acknowledged his mistakes and repented, I told him he was forgiven. He wasn't like some men that think they can't do any wrong and are always right. My Honey was willing to say "I am sorry."

I told Bro. Washington that I had had a heart attack in 1991. I didn't know when it happened. I became diabetic in 1992. I had had high blood pressure since 1986 and osteoarthritis in 1982. I also had been healed from Irritable Bowel Syndrome (IBS). Most people did not know I was sick. They didn't know about my health. It was not an open topic of discussion and I did not look sick.

Bro. Washington had good health. His blood pressure was only mildly elevated. He kept it in a good range by exercising. I could not exercise because of my back. The doctors said that my x-rays and MRI's showed that I had degenerative disk disease, spinal stenosis and sciatic nerve disease.

I had been under so much stress, as you can tell from reading my story you can understand. I experienced pain throughout my life. Some of you have probably been under more stress than I have. It may not have affected you as severely as it did me. Some who were not as stressed as I was, have literally let the stress kill them. Stress affects all of us differently. But never doubt for a second, it does affect us.

I told Bro. Washington that I had all of these ailments. I said "I do not want to be a burden on you or my children. I am asking the Lord to heal me. I want to spend some long healthy and happy years together." He agreed. Then he asked "When are we setting the date?"

I asked him to speak to his children again. He did. Some said "Daddy you don't need to marry." He told them "Y'all don't know what I need."

At that point I told him we couldn't get married. He wanted to know why not, I told him I was not going to bring confusion between him and his children. He said it did not matter. I told him to sit down and listen to me. I told him "It does matter. They are your children. They were in your life first. I want us to be able to have dinners and it to be a loving atmosphere with everyone enjoying each other, visiting with each other without there being any strain."

I did not understand their behavior but I wanted him to know why we couldn't marry under the circumstances. I thought it would be too much strain on both of us. I asked him if they thought I was going to "eat him up."

We both laughed.

He again asked me "When is the date?" I told him I didn't know. He said you need to know. I asked him to help me pray. He said he had prayed. I suggested we continue to pray on it.

I had hurt my knee in the bus accident coming from Michigan. It began to hurt really badly. When we had communion at church I could no longer bend down on my knees. I had to stand or sit down, mostly sit.

When the spirit came upon me and I started to praise the Lord, I could not shout (dance in the spirit) for the pain. The doctor put me on a new medication that gave me some relief. At first he told me to just not bend my knee and to be careful praising. It was hard not to praise the Lord.

One day in prayer and meditation, the Holy Spirit said to me again "Alfred is your husband." I asked the Holy Spirit about Alfred's children. The Holy Spirit said I didn't have anything to worry about."

The Holy Spirit said, as clear as a bright sun shiny day, "I am taking care of the children!" I didn't know exactly what that meant but I did understand the situation was covered under His Grace.

I told Bro. Washington what had happened during my meditation and prayer. He was so happy and so was I. So we set a date for May 17, 1997 at 3PM for our wedding at Long Cane AME Church in Abbeville, SC. At first we had thought about 1PM right after church services. I thought 3PM sounds like a good time. I talked it over with Bro. Washington.

He said 12 Noon would suit him. I asked how about we have our wedding and have it at 3PM. He said he didn't have any money for a wedding. I said to him politely "Did I ask you for any money?" I had a little money saved and was planning a small wedding. One day he came by and gave me $100 toward the wedding. I put it on the flowers. This was February, 1997 when we decided to get married in May, 1997.

My children were excited. Ojetta said "Mama I will be there!" Ivey was in Atlanta, GA. She said "Mother I will be there." Harry and his wife Virginia lived in Miami, FL. They said they would be there. Shirley Ann lived in Greenwood, SC. I knew she would lovingly attend. My Washington family and friends in Greenville, SC were so happy for us.

I felt so sad that his children did not support us more. I wanted them to be very happy for us too. I knew that they had had a good and loving mother. I also knew I couldn't be their mama but I had hoped to be the "other mother" or a good friend. Someone important in their lives, not "that old thing", but a pleasant, positive, loving person in their lives.

They came to the wedding but were distant. I said "Lord, you told me not to worry, but this is hard. Please let them see that I love him and I will be very good to him."

So we, Mrs. Georgia East and I, made plans for the wedding. I went to Greenville to order a wedding gown.

Two weeks later they called to tell me that the dress was on back order and it would be in in two weeks. After that two weeks past, Mrs. East and I went to Greenville to try on the dress. It was dark beige - the wrong color. So they sent it back and reordered it in ivory.

Two weeks later we went back to try on the ivory dress. It was too small. I could not believe this so they had to reorder the right size. By then we were in to the month of March.

I had to get a caterer for the wedding, order the flowers, get the tuxedos for my soon to be husband and his sons, who were going to be ushers and groomsmen and talk to the Pastor. Five of his sons and two daughters were in the wedding.

I had to decide on the menu and what kind of flowers I wanted. I also had to decide on the director. The director would lead the wedding rehearsal, make sure everyone knew what they were supposed to do and be in their proper places at the right time. I wanted things done decently and in order.

Three days before Ojetta was to arrive, I received a call from Greenville stating that my wedding dress was no longer in stock. I thought "Oh no!" Mr. Petersen drove Bro. Washington to Greenville to pick Ojetta up from the airport.

Ojetta said she spoke to Bro. Washington, shook his hand and asked him "Mr. Washington, are you going to be good to my Mama?" He told her he was going to be as good to me as he knew how to be.

Ojetta said if his answers had not suited her, she was going to be on the next flight back to Michigan. Ojetta said he did not hesitate to answer her questions in a very positive way. She was happy and she liked him right away. He liked Ojetta immediately also.

When Ojetta arrived in Edgefield, where I was living, we were so happy to see each other to say the least. She said "Mama I am so glad you got your dress." I told her the dilemma about the dress. She was disappointed, but quickly said, "We'll find you the perfect dress!"

She arrived in Edgefield on Wednesday. We went to Augusta, GA that evening, looking for a dress. I talked to one of my friends and told her what was going on with my dress. She told me to go on Broad Street in Augusta to a boutique called Sho Ane's Design Studio.

We went there and I tried on several dresses. They were all beautiful with a handsome price. They had a good selection of lovely jewelry to choose from. Their hours of business were from 10AM to 6PM. I drove Ojetta and myself to Augusta, GA. We arrived at 5PM.

The shop owner Ms. Sho was so kind and friendly. I had the best consultant. I cannot remember her name. Ms. Sho was assisting her. They helped me find my dream dress to marry my handsome groom.

For the wedding my colors were peach, ivory and light beige. They did have some dresses in beige and ivory. They weren't my size – either too small or too large. Then this beautiful peach dress caught my eye. It was too large and needed some alterations. So we left there after 7PM. We had to go back the following evening, a Saturday, to try it on and pick it up.

Ojetta and I decided Sho Ane's was the place I was supposed to go to for my dress. I recommend it highly. Our footsteps are ordered by the Lord! Ojetta and I had both been disappointed when she arrived that I did not have my dress. It was no fault of mine but still I had wanted that accomplished before Ojetta arrived. But the Lord had a better plan. He always does!

Ojetta and I were tired and hungry when we left Sho Ane's so we stopped in North Augusta, SC and ate at the S&S Café. The food was good as always. Ojetta stated if we were not so hungry we could go sit down and order our food. I told her this place was just fine, we were in no rush so we decided to dine in. I enjoyed eating there.

I had fried chicken, carrot salad, and turnip greens. Ojetta had fried chicken, tossed salad and green beans. We both ordered desert – apple pie. The food was so good. We took our time and arrived back home after 10PM.

I was getting married the next Saturday. My family and I were happy. I was asking the Lord to let his children know that I loved their daddy and would not in any way mistreat him.

Not a one of my husbands would tell you I mistreated them and I have had three - my children's father Deacon Norman Brown, after his death Steward David Edmunds, after our divorce I married Steward Alfred Washington. In the Baptist church they have "Deacons," in the A.M.E. (African Methodist Episcopalian of the C.M.E. Christian Episcopalian Methodist) they have Stewards.

One of my husbands told me I was too good for him. Guess which one? You are right if you guessed the second husband David Edmunds. I told him that I didn't know any other way to treat him but good.

As I have said David Edmunds was a good kind-hearted person who just needed to be single. We did have some wonderful times together but apparently not enough. I thank God we remained friends, who needs enemies. Divorced or not, forgive others as others have forgiven you and God has forgiven us all – in Jesus name! I am grateful for the love of Jesus and his forgiveness and his benefits.

My daughter Ojetta and I spent the rest of the week, really Monday and Tuesday, making sure everything was in order, I had my dress. The groom had his tuxedo. The best man was Steward Clyde Wims. He and the sons James (Nick), Benjamin (Ben), George (Jug Head) and Stanley (Joe Buddy) also had their tuxedos.

The music, food, programs and flowers were in place. Ojetta and I went to Belks and purchased a beautiful Ivory dress for her. Thursday night we had manicures and pedicures. Friday night was the wedding rehearsal. I had a hair appointment Saturday at 7AM.

Ojetta picked up a stereo system at 12:30PM and took it to the church, Long Cane AME. Pastor James Stokes, Bishop Emanuel Spearman did the wedding ceremony and Ojetta sang, "God and God alone". We had our granddaughter Nikki Butler sing "We're Going to Make It" at the wedding.

Everyone was supposed to be at the church by 1PM with the wedding at 3PM. The reception was going to be at 5PM at the National Guard Armory in Abbeville, SC. Rev. and Mrs. Rufus East served dinner at 8PM. My husband and I (WOW! I could finally say my husband) left the Easts' at 11:30PM. The friends and guests from Edgefield, SC, Greenville, SC and Greenwood, SC left before we did.

We honeymooned at the hotel in Greenwood, SC for two days. Then to the elegant Grand Regency Hotel in Augusta, GA for seven days. (Ojetta and I had checked out the rooms. They had beautiful rooms and it was hard to decide. The room had a refrigerator in it and we stocked it with food.)

Ojetta arrived on the Wednesday before the wedding. She stayed in my house in Edgefield while Bro. Washington and I were on our honeymoon. She returned to Michigan after two weeks.

The next Sunday, my husband went to church. I was still tired from the wedding, the reception and the dinner. We had a trunk load of gifts in the trunk of the car. My husband and I got into bed after midnight.

My husband was an earlier riser than I was. I had some food cooked that he heated up for his breakfast and I made coffee. So he was good to go to church service. After church we went to dinner at The Olive Garden.

Aunt Mary had us for dinner on Friday and Sunday. Aunt Mary had not been pleased that I was getting married. She felt I should have stayed married to David Edmunds because he had a big fine house and was more financially stable.

I reminded her that I had not married David because he had a big fine house or the things he could provide, but because I loved him. I believed, and still believe, that life is so much more than material possessions. Life is about being connected to the spiritual part of life and being led by something greater than yourself. Life is about being able to love and receive love. It is about being honored and treated well.

I knew that the Lord had spoken to me and sent Alfred Washington to be my husband. I was going to obey God rather than man. I knew that there are blessings in obeying God. Glory to God the most High!

We had our first disagreement when the doctor told him his blood hemoglobin was a little low about three months after we married. I cooked cabbage, beef liver, corn bread and beets. The beet juice had gotten on the cabbage and he felt it looked unappetizing. He said "You have messed my food up."

I was hurt. I said from now on he should cook his own food. I had to apologize to him later because I did not mean that at all.

He said "Baby, you didn't know." I told him from then on I would know. That's how we handled our disagreements – no arguing, fussing or cussing. It was so smooth for us. Thank the Lord!

The beginning of our marriage we had to go every six months to have polyps removed from his colon. He had had a colonoscopy which revealed non-cancerous polyps. A follow-up exam was required every six months. Each time he returned for an exam, more polyps were found and had to be removed. After two years of this I asked the Lord to please let this be yearly. He heard and answered my prayers. The doctor advised him we only had to come back once a year. Praise God!

We lived in Edgefield for one year after we married. I had been staying there for two years before we married. Then we moved into my brother-in-law's house in Greenwood. This was my first husband's brother - James and my sister-in-law Bennie Brown. It was a very nice place. My husband and I were very happy in Greenwood.

Some of the children said that my husband and I did not have a normal sexual marriage – whatever that meant. For the record, my husband had a strong sexual desire and natural desire. We had no desire to experience anything new. We stuck to the old fashion way, if you get my drift. He did not need Viagra. Mind you, when we married he was 82 years old. I said earlier my husband was strong in every way. His stamina and vitality were amazing.

One Sunday, in church school, the teacher had an awesome lesson as she always did. This Sunday we were talking about relationships. Each of us had input in the discussion. I told them when my husband walked into a room my eyes lit up and when he would put his arms around me, embracing me I literally felt like I could fly. Our marriage was close to a perfect one.

I had knee surgery a year after moving to Greenwood on October 28, 1998. I had put it off for ten years, dreading it. I had heard about these specialists in Augusta, GA. I talked to my orthopedic surgeon Dr. Christian. He did a wonderful job on my knee. He told me he could do my surgery as well as anyone and could give me the best care any one could. That was exactly what I wanted to hear. I had several blood clots and he advised me to have a green leaf filter implanted to keep any blood clots from passing into my body.

In 1999 I was having chest pains while Ivey and I were out shopping. I told my daughter how I was feeling. We called my husband. They both agreed I should go to the emergency room. My husband told my daughter to take me and he would be there when we arrived. They admitted me and did many heart tests.

My cardiologist was Dr. Thomas Pritchard. He came and gave me the results. I had no blockages. I told him that in 1991 I had 30% heart blockage. He told me I didn't have any blockage now. I asked him if he was sure.

About an hour later he came back with Dr. James Smith the head cardiologist. Dr. Smith told me and my husband that I had no blockage and everything looked good. He looked at my husband and told him "Don't trade her in! She has a lot more mileage on her."

I was in the hospital for four days. I was glad to go home. My husband was glad too. My children were shouting to hear the good news. So now my right knee was fixed after a long period of recuperation and my heart was better. Thank you Jesus!

I joined my husband's church. He was a class leader. Some of the other class leaders thought I might not want to be in my husband's class. I told them I would be honored to be in my husband's class. We worked together well as I knew we would.

When he returned for a checkup they discovered my husband's polyps had returned. He had the polyps removed, then he had gall bladder surgery. Both surgeries went well.

My husband was a praying man. If I had a pain he would lay his hand on me and pray. I would feel better. Thank you Jesus for your healing touch. After he and I were married I began to heal from all my illnesses. If my husband had pain, I would lay my hands on him and pray also.

While living in Greenwood my daddy Jimmy Joe Oglesby died in June, 2000. He had been diagnosed with pancreatic cancer in February. He was buried on my birthday June 12, 2000.

My husband had met my father several times and they got along really well. Dad was not perfect but he was kind and thoughtful. The first time he met my husband was when he came down to his brother's, Otis Oglesby's, funeral in 1998. He was not able to attend our wedding.

In November, 1998 I asked my daddy if he was saved. He shocked me when he said he wasn't sure. My husband and I looked at one another and we knew he wasn't saved. So we began to talk to him about the plan of salvation. He accepted Christ right then and there. Hallelujah! Thank you Jesus! I will see him in Heaven some sweet day! That Thanksgiving in 1998 my first cousin, Jean Simpkins cooked dinner and other cousins prepared food.

When we went to Baltimore for the funeral we went by train. My husband did not want to fly. I was not flying then either, the way I do now. I used to really like riding the bus. Greyhound was my main ride LOL!

We returned from Baltimore on Wednesday and my husband went to work at West Carolina Telephone that Thursday. I asked him if he wanted to rest but he said he wasn't tired.

One day the doorbell rang and this gentleman asked if we knew our house was in foreclosure? I said "What? Oh, no!" My husband was sitting in the den. I went to tell him. I thought, how he is going to take this. He did not take it any better than I did. We both were just flabbergasted. The house had been owned by my brother-in-law James and his wife Bennie. Both were deceased and an executor was responsible for paying the mortgage

We rented the house from the executor. I called him to find out what was going on. He stated that it was not true that the property was being foreclosed. I believed him. Someone had made a mistake. The realtor came back with a for sale sign in hand. He told us we could buy the house or we had thirty days to move.

We were so upset, putting it mildly. My husband said he wanted to go get his gun and shoot the man that caused the foreclosure. I told him that would not work. That action would only get him in trouble and cause heart ache and pain to someone else.

I told him God would help us. I told him it might not feel like it; we might not be able to see it; but God had not brought us this far to leave us. He said that I was right but we had to pray, pray and pray.

The executor subsequently lost all of his other properties and suffered many personal tragedies.

I wanted to get another house or buy this house. The Holy Spirit said to me you need to live in Abbeville in your husband's home, where he lived with his first wife and raised their children. I didn't want to live there. My daughter in Michigan told me that she could purchase a home for us and we would just have to pay the note. I thought that would be great.

The Holy Spirit again told me that I should live in my husband's home. Ojetta called again saying she would make the down payment. She told me to have things appraised, do everything – insurance and taxes – and to just make the note. I said wonderful.

We went looking at other homes. We learned the house we were in had something majorly wrong with the water line. The Lord spoke to me again saying, "You have to live with your husband in his home in Abbeville." So I had to be obedient.

We moved there in 2003 and stayed there until February 11, 2005. The house in Abbeville was in a state of serious disrepair. Washington and I were both depressed to be there.

My husband worked at West Carolina Telephone on Tuesdays and Thursdays and really enjoyed it. I was glad when we moved from Edgefield to Greenwood even though I had a lot of family in Edgefield, SC.

My sweet husband had approximately a 75 minute drive to work. Moving to Greenwood his drive was cut down to 15 minutes. He told me after we moved he was glad to be out of Edgefield. I asked him why he hadn't told me before. He said because it wasn't that bad. The trip to his job from his home in Abbeville was only five minutes.

I told him the Holy Spirit had begun to reveal to me that the distance was getting a bit far for him to drive while we were living in Edgefield. Then I began to pray about it. He said the Holy Spirit is right. I told him the Holy Spirit is always right and truthful.

My husband and I could find humor in the strangest things. It is important to be able to have humor in our relationships, friendships and, by all means, in our marriages. Christians can have good clean fun.

I like to have fun. I use to be so stiff and up tight. My first husband would tease me about it. Eventually I began to loosen up and enjoy the fun and laughter. My first husband Deacon Brown, the father of my children, would tell you he would tease me. He would say "Sugar babe lighten up I am only kidding." I began to loosen up and enjoy the fun and laughter.

One day my husband, Bro. Washington was having a problem with his stomach. He went to his primary doctor who sent him to a specialist. The specialist said he needed surgery for an intestinal blockage.

Two weeks later he was scheduled for the surgery. Ojetta came from Michigan to be with us for the surgery. She had been there the month before but said she would return when "Daddy Washington" had his surgery. The surgeon had to remove part of his large intestine.

We had him at the hospital at 6AM. About 7:30AM it was announced over the "P.A." that a tornado was approaching the hospital. Ojetta and I began to pray. I am sure there were others at the hospital praying also.

The storm was very bad. The lights went out for a short period of time before the emergency generator kicked in. Our prayers worked. The storm was cancelled. There was no tornado in our area.

My husband had a rough time recovering from his surgery.

One night I started not to stay. One of his daughters had said "You don't need to stay. Daddy is doing good." And he was. The Holy Spirit however was telling me to stay. So you know what I did.

That night he was so sick. I had to keep calling the nurse. He had severe pain. Later he started vomiting and his temperature went up. He began to hallucinate. Then he calmed down. I thanked the Holy Spirit that I was there. The nurses were busy and would not have known.

My husband was in the hospital thirteen days. On the twelfth day my pop, Pop Lewis, died. That's the only night I did not stay. One of his sons stayed with him that night.

Pop Lewis was the man who had lived with my mother for eighteen years. About two years after my mother died he got married. He was happy that I approved of him getting married. He would come to Calhoun Falls, SC to visit my husband and I. We would visit him and his family in Greenwood, SC.

I called him "Pop Lewis". I loved him like a second father. He had been close to my second husband, David Edmunds, as well. Every Saturday morning Pop Lewis would come to visit us. We looked forward to his visit.

I remember a year earlier when I was doing home visits, as a nurse in Laurens, SC I stopped by Pop Lewis and his wife's home and began to talk to them about the Lord. His wife was already a Christian. I asked him if he would like to become a Child of God. He said immediately "I sure would." He received Jesus that day. Hallelujah!

A year after that day, Pop Lewis had a stroke. He could not use his left side. He had therapy for a while then the therapy was discontinued. The Holy Spirit told me to drive from Edgefield, SC to Greenwood, SC three times a week for a month then twice a week for another month to help him continue with his physical therapy exercises. It helped him a great deal to build up his muscles. I am thankful for being obedient to God! I encouraged his other family members to continue with the exercises. Years later he got to the place where he could not eat and the doctor had to insert a feeding tube.

Pop Lewis' wife became ill. I would go visit them both. I would take them juices. Pop's favorite juices were prune and apple. He liked to have prune juice before the feeding tube. I called his wife Mother Inez. She was so sweet and nice to Pop Lewis. I brought her favorite juices, cranberry and orange, also. They were always glad to see me. I would sing and have prayer with them. Mother Inez became diabetic so I had to discontinue bringing her juices.

As I was saying my husband was in the hospital thirteen days and on the twelfth day of his hospital stay in Greenwood my Pop Lewis died.

I had so much to do concerning the funeral. I called his daughter in Atlanta, GA Effie Turner. She was my Pop Lewis' daughter but she was always like a sister to Cherry and I. My mother treated her like a daughter too. I had to get in touch with Pops' sister and other family members.

My husband came home the day after Pop Lewis died. I was taking care of my husband while planning Pop's funeral.

Pop Lewis' step daughter would not use the insurance money to bury him. They wanted a cremation but Pop had told me he did not want a cremation. His wife had been cremated but he did not want that. I had promised him, if I was still alive, he would not be cremated. There is not a thing wrong with cremation. In fact, I use to feel the same way as Pop but since his death I have done research on it. Now I want to be cremated and have expressed this to my family.

I didn't have insurance for Pop Lewis. Our church family and friends were so good to us. My nephew Reggie came with his mother Effie to the funeral. Effie, her cousin Anthony and I took it upon ourselves to pay for Pop Lewis' funeral.

Before my Pop Lewis died the Holy Spirit told me to release him. I couldn't. I would not talk to anyone about it. After about a month I told my husband and my children. They told me that they knew it was hard but I had to release him to heaven. A week later my husband asked me how I was doing at releasing Pops? I told him not good. He said I had to do what the Lord was telling me. He said Pop Lewis was suffering because I would not release him. I knew my husband was telling me the truth.

So the next couple of days I went to see him and released him. It was very hard. I had lost my father two years ago and now I had to release my other dad. He died peacefully about a week later. I said, "Lord help me and give your servant strength."

Our granddaughter Melissa Lee stayed with my husband while we attended the funeral. Some of the flowers were missing. My cousin had forgotten them. I was upset about that. My brother Bishop Emanuel Spearman did the eulogy. Rev. Fannie Higgins Clark, Rev. Camiller Simpkins, Rev. Rufus East, Minister Georgia East and Rev. Thomas Duncan also presided at the funeral.

Our daughter Ann Coleman was in charge of serving the food. My daughter Shirley Ann was with me. I gave Pop Lewis one of my plots in Evening Star Cemetery. We went back home and had dinner. Ann did a good job in serving everyone.

A month after my Pops died, Effie lost one of her sons, Reggie – the one that came with her to the funeral. She and her husband Larry had another son named Ronnie. It was heart breaking for Effie when her son Reggie was killed. She had to be responsible for Reggie's funeral. Weeks later her cousin, that helped with Pop Lewis' funeral, came down ill and was no longer able to work.

I was still taking care of my husband while we were preparing for Reggie's funeral. When I took my husband back to the surgeon for a checkup, the doctor was so surprised at how well he was doing. He said he had seen men in their thirties who did not do half as well as my husband. He told us my husband that he could go back to work in three months. Washington was back to work at West Carolina Telephone Co. in one month and doing well. Glory to God!

We were living in Abbeville in 2003. We stayed there in my husband's home until we moved into an apartment in Greenwood, SC. We finally had to move from Abbeville because the house was so poorly insulated. It was terribly hot in the summertime and freezing cold in the winter.

My daughter Ivey took me to look at many apartments. Ojetta and Connie went on the internet from their home in Michigan and would send Ivey information to give me. The one I chose was the last one Ivey thought I would choose because it was smaller than the others I had looked at. Yet, it had its own driveway and private entrance so it looked more like a condo and was easier to carry packages and groceries to the door.

Some of the other apartments, I had looked at, had stairs that would be hard for me to climb. I knew my husband didn't want to climb any stairs either. Some apartments were too far for him to drive to West Carolina Telephone company and some had a lot of traffic. So I thought 616B Trakas Ave was the logical choice.

Washington called me "Baby." He did not call me Lillian and I did not call him Alfred. All I ever had heard him called, as far as a nickname, was "Mr. Nina." One day after we were married I overheard him telling someone that his name was Alfred not Nina.

I said "Honey they have been calling you that for a long time." He said yes that was true but he did not like it. I was in shock and asked him if he knew how he got that name – Nina. He told me his mother said one day he started walking and someone said "here comes little Nina" and that's what the family started calling him but he never liked the name.

We were now living back in Greenwood. My husband had to have eye surgery. One morning when we were going to church he could hardly see to drive. I took him to the eye doctor the next day. He had a cataract that needed to be removed.

The day it was removed I had to feed him because he had one eye bandaged. He couldn't see out of the other because of a childhood injury. I enjoyed feeding my sweetie because he couldn't do it himself. The next day I took him back to the doctor to get the bandage and stitching removed. He did very well.

By this time I had joined "Living Waters Church of Worship" in Greenwood. The only people I knew there were Rev. Fannie H. Clark and her family. I told her the Lord was leading me there. I did not know the pastor. I just called her one day and told her the Holy Spirit was leading me to her church.

Rev. Clark told me they would be happy to have me as a member. She and I have been friends for a long time. I knew her mom and dad. I had worked with her brother, Hayward Higgins at Self Regional.

I joined Living Waters Church of Worship in March, 2005. The people were so kind and friendly. The pastor was Clara O. Barnes. Her husband was Deacon Herbert Barnes. He began to call me Mother. I was so honored. The entire congregation began to call me Mother Washington. I was so proud.

I claimed Deacon Barnes for my son. Deacon Saxon asked me to be his spiritual mother also. I claimed Evangelist Fannie Higgins Clark's daughter, Sanquienetta Williams for my god daughter. Deacon Barnes and Sanquienetta was a God thing. The Holy Spirit revealed them to be my children. How good is this? They accepted to be a part of my family. I told everyone that the Lord had blessed me with a new son and goddaughter. I was praising the Lord and thanking him.

One of my neighbors, Sis. Cornelia Reid would attend church with me every Sunday. She enjoyed it. We had a wonderful church school, worship service and bible study. Bible study was on Tuesday night. The pastor was an awesome preacher, teacher and prophet.

After the Holy Spirit lead me to join Living Waters Church of Worship my husband said he couldn't understand why I was leaving Long Cane AME church. I really enjoyed going with him. I always believed that husband and wife should worship together – my opinion. He kept saying he didn't understand my decision to change churches.

He asked me how Rev. Johnson and I got along. I told him we got along well. He said he thought we did. I told him everything at Long Cane AME was going just fine but the Holy Spirit had called me to go to Living Waters Church of Worship.

My husband told me he was not going to Living Waters Church of Worship with me. I told him I wasn't asking him to leave his church. I reminded him that the only reason I was leaving was because the Holy Spirit said so. Another night he told me again that he did not understand my decision. I said "Honey, if you have any questions please talk to the Holy Spirit about His decision for me."

My husband must have had that conversation with the Holy Spirit because he stopped talking to me about it and he even went with me when I preached. Some Sundays he went with me when I wasn't preaching. I was surprised that he went with me from time to time. He enjoyed it when he went.

My pastor and everyone at the church enjoyed his presence. Some members even called him Dad because I was one of the church mothers. I went with him to Long Cane for special events. I did not nag or bug him about going to church with me. All I did was pray and ask the Lord for peace between us concerning this situation for the Lord is not the author of confusion but of peace, love and a sound mind.

One week I got a cold and cough. I felt so badly. Ivey visited me on Saturday and asked Washington to stay home from church with me, that Sunday, because I was very sick. He had told her that I just had a little cold. Ivey told him that if he were sick that I would have stayed with him.

My husband went to work that Tuesday. Ivey came by to check on me. She asked where my husband was. I told Ivey that she knew my husband liked his job. Ivey walked over to my neighbor's apartment, Sister Reid, a couple of doors down from me. When she returned she said "Mother we are taking you to the doctor." She said I needed to go to the E.R. I told her I would rather go to my doctor in Edgefield.

Ivey had already called the doctor's office and told them I would be coming in. I called my husband on his cell phone and told him Ivey and Sister Reid were taking me to the doctor. I told him that I would see him when I returned home.

I was coughing so much that I would be out of breath. My doctor was off that day but the doctor who was in the office had attended me before. Had I known my doctor was off that day, I most likely would have gone to the ER. The doctor they had on call was very nice. After the examination he ordered a breathing treatment. He was going to lunch but would check on me afterwards. He said if the treatment did not help he would need to admit me into the hospital.

I thought "Oh no!" I had told my husband that I would see him at home. When the doctor returned from lunch he told me he could hear me wheezing as he was coming down the hall. He said I was sounding like a freight train. I was admitted to room 120. Ivey went to my home and told Washington. They returned together to visit me in the hospital that evening.

The next morning when the doctors made their rounds my doctor was with them. I was so glad to see her. She told me I had pneumonia in my left lung. I stayed in the hospital for six days.

I was very ill. One day I thought I saw my granddaddy all dressed up in his black suit, white shirt and black tie. He was tall and handsome. One day I was talking with my mother. Both had been deceased for many years. Another day my blood pressure was only 60/49. The nursing staff advised me not to get up and walk alone. My blood pressure dropped low because I was so ill. My body was working hard to fight off the pneumonia.

I was in the hospital for six days. My family was very supportive, visiting often, praying for me and offering words of encouragement.

Mrs. Georgia East asked me to come and stay with her family when I was discharged from the hospital. I had to think and pray on that and talk to my husband. I told him it would be better than having him trying to take care of me. I told him Mrs. East had volunteered her home and service. No one else had done that.

I told him to pray over it. Reverend and Mrs. East also wanted my husband to come and stay while I was there with them recovering. My husband said he was not going to the East's home but told me I could go if I wanted to. I told him then when I leave the hospital I would be going to Abbeville until I felt better. I said "You come see me Ok?" He said "Oh yea, I am coming to see you."

The doctor had me on Levaquin IV, an antibiotic that took my hair out and gave me tendinitis in my right arm. I could not use that arm for more than two weeks which was especially hard as I am right-handed.

I had long, beautiful, thick and healthy hair. I would cut it and it always grew back in a short period of time. That medication destroyed my hair. I was so upset and depressed about my hair loss. The side effects of some medication can be devastating. I was never told that medication might take my hair out or give me debilitating tendon pain. I better understood how women felt who have chemo or other treatments that take their hair out. A woman's hair is important to her, mine was certainly important to me. Every time I looked in the mirror I was reminded of what happened. My hair has never grown back and on some days I still grieve that. I decided I could not stay depressed about it, so I started wearing wigs, I had never worn a wig before. Thank God for wigs. Today I see the beauty in me, when I look in the mirror, wig and all!

I was discharged on a Sunday afternoon. Mrs. East had everything prepared so nicely for me at her lovely home. God is good!

My husband came to see me that following Monday. He spent the night. That Tuesday he was going to work at West Carolina Telephone. Tuesday morning his car would not start so Rev. East took him to work. I am glad he was there.

After work Rev. East picked my husband up from work. My husband called a mechanic to check the car. The mechanic couldn't check the car until Wednesday. They had to order the part and it would not be delivered until Thursday. Rev. East drove my husband to work again on Thursday. My husband would not have had transportation to work that week if he had stayed in Greenwood and hadn't come to visit me on that Monday. God always looked out for our good.

On Friday the mechanic had the car repaired. My husband told me he did not feel well that morning. I checked his blood pressure and it was 110/60. I told him his vital signs were good and he was probably upset about the car. He did not like to spend money.

I told him to just take it easy. He wanted to return to Greenwood to get more clothes. I asked Rev. East if he would take him and offered to pay for the gasoline. People can't drive their cars on air. So thank the Lord my husband did not have to drive while he was not feeling well.

That Saturday morning Rev. East cooked breakfast, Sister East slept a little later. We enjoyed the breakfast. I was in the shower and my husband came into the bathroom to shave. We both finished about the same time.

I had put my robe on when he turned from the mirror to walk out of the bathroom. He ran into the side door. I ran towards him. By that time he was out of the bathroom in the hallway. He was falling down towards the floor. I ran to him, trying to hold him up, calling for Reverend and Sister East. As he went down towards the floor, I held his head and kept it from hitting the floor.

Reverend and Sister East told me to let him lay down on the floor. The Holy Spirit told me not to let him lay flat on the floor. We got him on the sofa and I called 911. Then I called our children to give them a report. The emergency responders took him to the hospital. I felt bad because I could not go with him because I still had pneumonia.

Sister East went to the hospital with them while Rev. East stayed with me. Our children headed to the hospital. I called my pastor, Rev. Barnes. She came to the house. We hugged and prayed for my husband. Later our son Stanley and Minister East returned with my husband. I was so glad to see him and he was glad to be back with me. I couldn't wait to hear the diagnosis. The Emergency Room doctor said that the new blood pressure medicine his doctor had put him on had his heart beating too slow.

He did not go to church Sunday, the next day. Rev. East and his family went to church. Sister East cooked dinner before she left. Minister East is a very good cook. She had been serving some delicious food to us each day.

My husband said "Baby, you know what? I had planned to come see you, spend the night and not come back. I was upset because I wanted you to come home but you were just looking out for me. And the East's have been looking out for both of us." I was in shock and said "You had decided to come see your sick wife one time and that's all?" With tears in his eyes, he said, "That's right."

I reminded him that Sister East and Rev. East had made him welcome to come with me from the beginning. He said he knew that but he had wanted me to come home. He added that other family folk had said I needed to come home also. I asked him what family folk and he said his family.

He said he hadn't been thinking about me but about himself. He went on to say that he now knew he wouldn't have been able to take care of me and the others that were doing all the talking weren't going to help. He hadn't wanted to tell me what was on his mind when he came to visit.

I told him I was so glad to see him when he walked through the door. He told me that God had known what was in his heart. He said "I had meanness in my heart. I got over here and my car wouldn't start. Rev. East took me to work for two days. Then I got sick and Rev. East took good care of me. Minister East took good care of you."

He said that God didn't like ugly and he needed to repent. I told him the devil makes us act ugly. Jesus said we reap what we sow. I told him the good thing or the right thing is that you did acknowledge that you were wrong and asked God to forgive you. When he did that my husband had made things right again with God. We both just hugged each other.

We stayed in the East's home for two months and were treated like royal guests. We went home to Greenwood in May, 2005. I was stronger when I arrived home. When I had to go back to the doctor in April, Sister East took me. My daughter Shirley Ann took me for my appointment in May at the office in Edgefield. At that appointment the doctor said the x-rays revealed my lungs were clear. Praise the Lord!

On our anniversary on May 17th, Ivey brought us both a plate from Gary's Restaurant. Mrs. East brought us a cake she had baked and ice cream - Breyers one of my favorites. We had a nice anniversary. Ivey, Sister East and Evangelist Clark gave us nice gifts for our anniversary. Shirley Ann came over and had a nice gift. Ojetta sent us a nice card with a monetary gift. My husband and I were so blessed and happy.

Most days I did not feel up to cooking. I always had the funds to buy our dinner. We cooked breakfast, then my husband or I went and got lunch and dinner. Sometimes we went together. Sometimes I would get a supply of cooked food, a variety, to last us a couple of days. We always had plenty to eat.

I am a diabetic and had to eat before I took my meds. I would fix my husband's plate before I did my own. My husband had a good appetite. When he got up from eating he was always satisfied.

Six months after we had returned home, my husband had severe pain in his abdomen. I drove him to the hospital myself. They could not find anything wrong.

The next couple of weeks he had the same pain. I drove him back to the Emergency Room. A female physician came in to check him immediately. She said he had a hernia. They prescribed medication and said if that didn't help he would require surgery to repair the hernia. Several weeks passed with no significant relief. They did the surgery. Afterwards he had to really take it easy.

By December he was back to work at West Carolina Telephone. I drove him to work the first two weeks. My husband was so strong. God had truly blessed him with good strong health. One morning after his hernia repair he was getting up and slid to the floor beside the bed. I tried to get him up to no avail.

I called Ivey and she came over with Darius her son. Somehow by the help of the Lord we, mostly Darius, got him up. I was thankful to God when we got my husband off the floor. I put some pillows under his head while we waited for my daughter and grandson to arrive. I laid down on his side of the bed and talked to him.

In May 2007, my daughter Ojetta called me about our family going to Myrtle Beach for Thanksgiving. I talked to Ivey and her family. They were all excited.

I told my husband. He said he didn't have any money for the beach. I asked him if he wanted to go for Thanksgiving with the family. He said yes. I told him I wanted to go also. So Ivey drove us in my car. My son-in-law Eddie, Ivey's husband, drove his van.

Ojetta flew in from Michigan. Connie, Ojetta's wife, drove to Cincinnati, OH and picked up her son Walter, his wife Chauna and their infant son, Walter IV. Another car full of close friends from Cincinnati followed them to Myrtle Beach. Ojetta flew to Myrtle Beach due to her closed head injury which made long car rides terribly uncomfortable.

Ivey did not enjoy her trip. She had a panic attack. I was not feeling well. I did not make it out of the hotel room, except to go to Thanksgiving dinner.

We left Greenwood on Monday November 20, 2007. We all had nice hotel suites, the hotel was right on the beach. One morning we had a fire drill. It was not easy for my husband and I to climb the stairs. Ojetta helped us. She called the front desk to ask if this was a real fire or just a drill. She told them she needed to know because of her parents. They told her it was a drill. We both felt so much better.

The hotel suites had two queen size beds, a sofa, dining area and kitchen. My husband and I had one bed. Ojetta spent one night with us. She and her wife Connie were in another suite. We had lots of room. We had reservations at a restaurant on Thanksgiving Day. There were twenty-two of us. The food was delicious. That was the only time I left the room the entire trip. We left the hotel on Sunday. I think everyone enjoyed themselves. It's wonderful to get away but better to get back home.

In December Ivey was still having anxiety attacks due to a hormonal imbalance that was diagnosed later. I took her to the emergency room. We were invited to my cousin Jean and her husband Alfonso Simpkins' in Edgefield, SC for Christmas dinner. She had asked me to bring green beans and Ivey to bring potato salad.

Ivey was too ill to make the potato salad so I made both dishes. I drove my husband and myself to Edgefield. We also took plates and napkins. I wanted to stay for dinner but my husband did not so we went back home. Jean fixed us nice plates. I had also called the restaurant to cook Christmas dinner for us. I knew that Ivey was not able to cook so I had food for our two families.

I went to Watch Night Service at Living Water's on New Year's Eve. I had ordered New Year's food from the restaurant – collards, black eye peas, stewed tomatoes and okra, meat loaf, corn bread, and sweet potatoes.

XXIII

Mr. Washington's Health Decline

I first noticed a change in my husband as early as October 2007. By 2008 I noticed my husband becoming more disagreeable and harder to please. In the past we could always agree to disagree but now I noticed he wanted to argue. This was not like him at all. He never argued or pouted like some of my husbands had.

He would speak his mind if we were discussing something. He would tell me how he felt then say "I'm finished with it. I have said all I'm going to say." Then he would tell me to pray over it and let him know what the Lord said. I can tell you honestly we did not argue. That is one of the things I loved about him and that he loved about me.

I was never unfaithful in any of my marriages. I praise God for that because it was Him that kept me faithful. But you know, I did have the opportunity to be unfaithful, just as he did. My motto is do unto others as you would have them do unto you.

When I married Bro. Washington I did not think about another love interest. He didn't either. He would tell me about other women wanting to date him. He would tell them he was married and didn't need anyone else.

One woman, who was recently widowed, had told him she needed a boyfriend and that I would never know. My sweet husband told me, he had told her, that he and God would know. Another time we were attending a surprise birthday party at a friend's house. We were all dressed up looking fine. My husband had on a suit looking all handsome.

This lady came up to me and said "your husband sure does love you."' I said yes he does. She wasn't telling me anything I didn't already know. When she walked away I asked my husband what was that all about? He said he would tell me later.

I wanted to leave then so I could hear the story. But we had just arrived at the birthday party and dinner. As soon as we got in the car he explained that woman was the widow who had wanted him to be her boyfriend. I thanked the Lord for a truthful, faithful and devoted husband.

I had begun to notice changes in my husband's behavior around Christmas when he did not want to go to my cousin's home in Edgefield for dinner.

That morning he was so fussy. I prayed for the Lord to help him feel better and to help me too. Looking back, when we went to Myrtle Beach for Thanksgiving I noticed his mind was changing. He just wasn't feeling his best at this time and it continued.

One Saturday I told Ivey and my husband that I was going to get some herbal supplies, eggs, bread, coconut milk and something else from Emerald Farm. Ivey said she would pick me up and drive me. I was happy. I had already ordered the groceries that Friday. I asked my husband if he could think of anything he needed. He told me I had gotten everything he needed yesterday.

I told him I knew Ivey was going to stop by Food Lion. I told him I would call him before we came home to check if he had thought of anything else. So when we came back by the store. I called him to see if he had thought of anything else we needed. He said that he hadn't thought of anything else.

When we got back to the house Ivey and my granddaughter Ebony came in to say good bye to my husband. They stayed for a minute. When Ivey said "We'll see you later pop!" he usually replied "Okay Baby." This time he didn't. I said "Honey, Ivey is saying she will see you later."

Instead of his usual reply he said "That's alright. It's going to be alright." I asked him what was wrong, He said "They say y'all trying to hurt me." I asked him who was the "Y'all" saying this. He said the Holy Spirit told him it was me, Ivey, Rev. Spearman and Ojetta. I said "Honey that's not the Holy Spirit! Those are lies from the devil."

He went on to say, "The Holy Spirit talks to you!" I said yes but the Holy Spirit always told me the truth. I told him I would never hurt him any more than I would hurt myself. Ivey heard what he had said. She was so hurt and upset.

Ivey and Cherry sat on the porch. Ivey told me she need to go home and lie down after taking something for her headache. I told her she couldn't leave me because I needed her here. I knew if she went home and got into bed I would not see her again that day. I felt bad for asking her but I knew something was dreadfully wrong as his demeanor and temperament were becoming extremely different.

I told my husband I was going to call the children. He asked me not to call his children. I told him I had to let them know what was happening. I couldn't believe all this was happening. I needed to lie down myself.

I called his daughter Ann but got no answer. Then I called Larsena. Larsena was the oldest and Ann was next to the oldest. Larsena said that she was going to get some of the others and come over.

Ivey kept asking how my husband could think that we would hurt him. I told her he was not himself and something was wrong. I hoped he could express his fears better to all of us after the children arrived.

Larsena, Ann and Betty came over. He told them the same thing he had told Ivey and I earlier. Cherry and Ebony, Ivey's daughters, were in the van waiting for their mother. After they saw how confused my husband was they got out of the car. Cherry sat on the porch with her mother. Ebony came in the house.

His children talked to him for a while. Larsena told him he did not see Ojetta or Bishop Spearman every day. I told them Bishop Spearman was so busy we hardly saw him although he did call and check on us. Ojetta was in Michigan. After talking with him for a while they left and said if I needed them to call.

When the sun began to set and it got dark he began to talk about smelling dope. He walked outside and said the smell of dope was strong. I told him I didn't know what dope smelled like. He told me I might not know how it smelled but he did and said I was bringing dope in the house. I told him I was not.

Then he said I treated him like a dog. I was so hurt, the least to say. I asked him what I had done to treat him so badly? He thought about it but couldn't tell me. I told him he couldn't find an answer because it was not true.

His strange behavior continued. Sometimes he would talk all night. Other times I would be asleep and he would awaken me and ask why I was so dirty. He would tell me he wouldn't treat a dog the way I treated him. I'd ask him "Honey what am I doing that is so dirty?" He'd think but could never find an answer. There was no answer.

I use to love to run my hand over his shaven head. After his brain disconnected he would say don't rub his head – even telling me "Don't rub my head!" On his good days, when his brain seemed connected, I would ask "Honey do you mind if I rub your head?' and he would say "Baby why do you have to ask me if you can rub my head.' He told me that when we married "this became your head."

We would laugh. I would think praise the Lord, he is getting better. Then the "disconnect" would start again. Every night it was the same thing. It was much like what people suffering from Sundowners syndrome experience. Symptoms can include mood changes, agitation, and confusion. Once in a while we would have a good night.

I talked to the children and told them I needed to take him to the doctor. I took him to his primary physician and then to a specialist. The doctors did an MRI. Larsena, Ann and I went to the doctor for his report. They stated my husband had dementia. I had suspected that but to hear the words was so disheartening.

He began to leave the stove on. He would hide his medications and accuse me of moving them. He told me not to cook for him anymore. I wasn't cooking that much any way but it got to the place where he didn't even want me to fix his plate. He tried to fix it himself and would drop food everywhere. His hands were so unsteady. I understood what was happening but it didn't make it any easier.

I did a lot of praying. I asked his daughters if they would keep him for a few days so that I could get some rest and sleep. They agreed. He went there for one night and came back the next day. He said he wasn't staying over there. They weren't mistreating him but he said he thought they were too noisy.

As time went on it got worst. I was not getting any rest or sleep. One day I went to get some groceries and asked him to ride with me. He said he was going to stay home. On my way to the store I started to feel a strange sensation in my chest.

I went into the store to get the items we needed. My husband has asked me to bring him some vanilla ice cream and pound cake. He also wanted peanut butter, crackers, oatmeal cookies, breakfast sausage and a few other things. I bought a lot of groceries.

I knew I needed to go to the Emergency Room and not return home immediately. The pain in my chest was getting worst. I thought it probably was my blood pressure and would get it checked out at the E.R. I thought they would check me out, give me some new meds and send me home.

I drove fast to the E.R. and stopped in front of the door. By then I was experiencing shortness of breath. I opened the car door and told them I was sick. They came and got me with a wheel chair. I wanted to be treated and released but I was admitted. I wanted to let my husband know what was going on so he would not worry.

The E.R. doctor said I was threatening to have a heart attack. Ivey came to the hospital with her husband. I told her about the groceries in the car. The ice cream had melted so she threw it out and bought some more for my husband. I asked his/our children to take my husband home with them until I got discharged from the hospital.

He was not safe in the house alone. I was also worried he would walk away or try to drive to the hospital and get lost. They took my husband back to Abbeville. That made me feel better not having to worry about him. Once I knew he was safe, I was content. Thank you Jesus.

I was in the hospital for five days. Ojetta called me and told me she was coming to be with me. I told her not to come but she told me she already had booked the flight for the next day. I was happy she was coming. I needed her help.

Ojetta called us every day, sometimes several times a day, to check on us and ask how we were and if we needed anything. Ojetta was faithful to make sure that I had assistance to help me when I needed it. She and Ivey kept in touch with each other to keep things running smoothly.

The doctor said my blood pressure was extremely high and my heart was beating much too fast. My shortness of breath was out of control. I had edema in my legs, feet and ankles because my heart was not pumping adequately. Ojetta came the day before I was discharged. I had a stress test, echo cardiogram and an EKG.

My husband came back the day after I was discharged. That night he told Ojetta to sleep with me because I had dope in the bedroom and he was tired of smelling it. I didn't say anything. Ojetta said "Daddy Washington, mama doesn't use drugs. She doesn't know how dope smells." He told her he knew that I didn't know what it smelled like but he did.

The next morning he said he was feeling hot. Ojetta got up to fix our breakfast. She came into the bedroom and told me my husband said he was hot all around his neck. I told her to get a wash cloth, wet it with cold water and put it around his neck. She proceeded to do what I had asked. He told her to take it off of him and said she was trying to choke him.

I wasn't feeling well but I got up to check on him. I asked him what was wrong. He told me Ojetta had tried to choke him. I asked Ojetta to explain what she had done and she did. Ojetta and I sat down with him and we tried to clarify what had actually happened.

I told him I had instructed her to put the wash cloth around his neck to help cool him off. By this time Ojetta was near tears seeing him acting so unlike himself, she knew that she was witnessing dementia like behavior as she had elderly clients before, but to see it in your own parent is difficult. We both understood he was not in his right mind.

After I got him calmed down, my husband wanted to go pick up some samples the doctor had for him at their office. Ojetta told him as soon as she had a shower she would go for him and pick up the medication. She also would get us some breakfast while she was out. He did not agree with that. I asked Ojetta if she would get dressed and go get the samples and then shower when she returned. While she was dressing my husband left the house.

I was so worried. Ivey and my son-in-love were at work. I called my daughter Shirley Ann. She had gone to take someone to the doctor. Ojetta asked me if I knew the name of his doctor and the medications. She told me I should call the doctor. I couldn't think because of all the medications I was taking but it came to me. I called the doctor's office and told them my husband was on his way to pick up samples of his medicine. I asked them to call me if needed.

Then I worried that he might get lost. Ojetta said she knew how I was feeling but I needed to try not to be stressed. She said "Mama. Let's pray." I told her I felt he had been gone long enough to be back by now. I called the doctor again. He said my husband had left about 15 minutes ago. Shortly afterwards his grey car pulled into the driveway.

When he returned home I could tell he was frustrated. I asked him if he was alright. He said yes and asked why I thought he wouldn't be. He said "You think I'm crazy! I ain't crazy!" I told him I knew he wasn't crazy. I asked him if he had gotten lost. As soon as I said it, I thought, why did I ask him that? My mind wasn't functioning the best in those days either. He began to argue with me. He told me we were all just low down and dirty. This hurt me so bad but I knew in my heart he did not mean what he was saying.

I asked him how we were mistreating him. He thought about it and couldn't say. After a while he settled down. I asked him if it was ok if Ojetta used his car to get us some breakfast. My car was in the shop being repaired.

He said that breakfast places were no longer serving breakfast. It was 11 AM I told him Shoney's and Cracker Barrel served breakfast all day. He thought about it and said she could use the car. He said Ojetta knew she was welcome to use his car. He seemed to be back with us mentally. I said "Thank you Jesus his mind is getting better.

Ojetta got our breakfast and cooked our dinner. She brought it to us. That night my husband started smelling dope again. He asked why I kept bringing dope into the house. I told him I hadn't. He said then Ojetta must have brought it. Ojetta told him she hadn't brought drugs into the house either and she didn't use drugs either. I told her he had been making these accusations for six months.

Ojetta asked me why I had not told her this had been going on for six months. I told her I hadn't because I thought it would get better. I told her I was going to talk to our children and tell them I was taking him to a specialist. She thought that was a wonderful idea. That night we could not sleep.

I talked to the children. They told their father that he needed to see the doctor. He said he was not going and told them he was not crazy. They told him they knew he was not crazy and he was only going in for a checkup.

I told him I thought he needed to go to the doctor too. He told me that I was crazy so I decided to keep quiet. He kept fussing. I knew something was terribly wrong. He was not one to fuss or hold a grudge. He was usually so kind, sweet and easy to live with.

Ojetta came to stay for a week but stayed for a month. I needed her with me so much. She could see I was not well myself and was also worried about my husband. A few weeks later he got up one morning and said he couldn't stay with me any longer. Besides accusing me of bringing dope into the house, he said I was moving his medications and hiding his shoes.

I again told him I had not brought drugs in to the house, moved his medicine or hid his shoes. I showed him where he had moved his medications from the medicine cabinet and put them behind the television. I told him I had found his shoes on my side of the bed.

He called his/our children from Abbeville and told them to come and get him. I thought they could talk to him and get him to stay in our home. Larsena (May she rest in peace), Ann and Betty came. He told them Ojetta and I had been hiding his things and he was tired of it. Ojetta and I could not convince him otherwise. By the time Ivey arrived she saw how upset I was with him leaving. The children said maybe he should go to Abbeville for a few days. I felt better hearing he wouldn't be gone long. When he walked out the door I just broke down.

Ivey decided not to go back to work that day. She and Ojetta were trying to keep me calm, not to get stressed as the doctor had ordered. They gave me something to eat. I didn't have an appetite but I needed to eat before I took my medications. Then they told me I needed to lie down. I was in bed for at least two weeks – in and out for longer than that. Ojetta stayed with me a little over two weeks after Washington left with his children before returning to Michigan. My family had to help me with my shower. I was so weak. I talked to my husband on the phone. It gave me some relief to hear his voice.

When he left in February he said he wanted to help me pay some of the bills. I appreciated that but knew he couldn't give me much as he had bills to pay also. He told me he wouldn't miss what he would be giving me. He said he wanted to do the right thing because he wanted to go to heaven when he died. I told him we both did.

He gave me money in March, April and May. It was not much but I was thankful. At the end of May, on May 30, 2008, he called me and said that "all my chaps" had been fussing all day. At first I wondered if this was just in his imagination but I later confirmed that his friends were actually telling him that. He said I had a man and didn't need his help. He added "So I am cutting you lose." My heart dropped! I told him the only man I had known since him was my Lord and Savior, Jesus Christ.

After my husband told me he was cutting me loose I was so devastated. My heart was so broken. Unless you've been in love the way we were, it is hard to understand how I could have been so devastated and how my heart was so severely injured. When I called to talk to him I was told he got upset whenever he talked to me. I didn't feel like that was the truth.

His family and those around him thought he was going to try to slip me some money. I was not calling him about the money. Although the money he gave me came in handy, I had never depended on that income. I just wanted to stay connected to him in some form or fashion.

I told him I would help with his clothes and buying his food. I told him he had to eat and stay warm in the winter and cool in the summer. One of the Abbeville children said to me that I should have come and picked him up but by then his mind was completely no longer with me.

His mind had gone back to his first wife and the times they were raising their children. He only had long term memories, no short term. I was no longer a part of his life or memory. I would have gone and picked him up if he would have gotten in the car with me. I loved him and love makes you want to do stupid things.

My concern was that he would come with me but get up during the night and try to walk back to Abbeville, get lost or worst. I was praying, asking the Lord to help me, to guide me and direct me. I felt as if my husband wasn't with me, that he was with his children and being taken good care of.

I told him one time he would not need to go to a nursing home. He asked me if I thought he would. I told him no because he had all of his children, his grandchildren and me to look out for him. Eventually he had to go in to a home which made me feel so bad. At that time, I was sick and needed assistance myself.

I believe that Washington's children wanted him to divorce me..

They knew he did not have the mind after he was diagnosed with dementia to make that decision. Before the dementia set in he and I stated we would never divorce and we didn't. I had told him in the beginning that whatever he owned, if I out lived him, should go to his children. I supposed they did not believe what I had initially stated.

I am a woman of my word. He had property that belonged to his children. I have property that will go to my children. The first marriage is different than any marriage after that regarding property and so forth. I was shocked and hurt when I was presented with the papers – talking about stepping on you when you are already down. Why did they hate me so? I was sick and my children were taking care of me. The Abbeville children said they would check on me but never did.

I'm sure there must have been a good reason he had to go to a nursing home. I know his children loved their daddy as I did. Hearing his family say that I got tired of him and put him out hurt so very much. They knew that was not the truth. I cried so much.

One of my friends told me his children had placed him in a nursing home. Although I was never told that I could not visit him, I did not want to see him in a nursing home.

I remember the night the Holy Spirit told me to stop worrying and let Him handle the situation. I said "Lord you got it! Take it and deal with it!" By then I had shingles from worrying about people talking about the situation with my husband not even knowing what was going on. I had shingles for a year. My family and church family were so nice to me. Thank you Jesus! When you are sick you need your family and loved ones.

Before I got over the shingles I had to have surgery under my arm. Then I had to have periodontal surgery. It was a lot going on with my health but I never stopped praying for my husband or loving him.

One evening this gentleman called to ask me out to dinner. I told him I was married and not at liberty to go out with him. He asked me how long it had been since my husband had left our home. He said he had heard that we were separated. I told him that I didn't consider myself separated. He said okay and told me to call him when I did consider myself separated from my husband.

The funny thing is he thought he had hung up his phone and I heard him tell someone "Man, that lady is crazy! Washington's been gone a year

I know and she's talking about she is not free to go out to dinner with me." I wondered why do they call a person crazy when they are doing what they think is the right thing to do.

In October, 2010 one of my friends called me from Abbeville. She asked how I was. I told her I had been worrying about my husband. She said she understood. I said "I told you he is in a home." She said that was right. Something in her tone didn't sound right to me. She knew how much my husband and I loved each other.

She asked if I was alone. I told her I was. I knew why she was calling but I couldn't or didn't want to hear the words. So I told her to call me back. I was going to call my daughter Ivey. When I called Ivey she was in the bed asleep. I asked my grandson to come over. When he came over I asked him to call my friend in Abbeville. He began to talk to her. When his eyes began to fill with tears I knew for sure. My grandson said "Mama Rene, I am spending the night with you." The next day Washington's daughter Anne called to tell me of his passing.

I just could not believe my sweet husband made his transition to heaven. I thought "Lord I am not ready to face this right now. Lord give us strength." I was concerned about Ebony, my granddaughter. She loved her pops, my husband, so much. I told them to sit down and tell her. I knew she would have many questions. When did it happen, how did it happen and why did it happen?

God is good and all the time God is good. My family, church family, friends and loved ones were so good to us during our time of bereavement. Yes we were separated but it was no fault of ours. This awful disease called dementia separated us physically but it did not change my heart at all. My husband was a good kind Christian gentleman.

My aunt Omegene Oglesby and her daughter Leola came from Royston, GA to spend the day with me. I had many friends visit the day of the funeral – so much food and prayer. My cousins from Augusta, GA Dorothy, Cynthia and Theodore came to visit me the following week. Ivey and her family met them at my house.

I did not attend the funeral. No one said I could not attended but I decided not to go. I wanted to talk to my husband while he was able to talk to me. I was not allowed to do that. Therefore, I did not want to see him laying there, lifeless and breathless. It would have hurt me too much.

I prayed that he would understand my position. I knew by the Holy Spirit I was right. I know where he is buried but have never visited his gravesite.

My daughter Desmi was with me during the funeral and after my husband's home going. Desmi is my spiritual daughter. We met at Living Waters Church of Worship in 2005. I was one of the mothers of the Church. She and I became closer and eventually became like mother and daughter. She, Ojetta and Ivey are close, like sisters.

Desmi came to visit me every evening after she left her career at Burton Center. She came at least for three months afterward. It was a blessing to me. So many people visit you the first week then they slack off but Desmi did not do that for which I am eternally grateful. She is so faithful towards me and I love her like a daughter.

My husband gave me many visitations – a spiritual experience - after his death. If I was sad he would come and just embrace me. His spirit communicated with me visibly and audibly.

One night he gave me a visitation saying not to shed any more tears unless they were tears of joy. I thought "tears of joy" you are no longer here my beloved husband. How can I possibly shed tears of joy? His spirit said "you will see."

One day Ivey and Ebony came to see me. I was singing "Oh How I Love Jesus" with tears flowing down my face. I thought this is what my husband's spirit was talking about. My husband said to me "You were good to me and you were good to my children." I thanked him and told him I had always wanted them to be my children too! I never wanted them to think of me as "that old thing" or say "I can't stand her." I just wanted to be a loving person in their lives. That's what I had always wanted from the beginning.

I have so many children, some call me mother, mama, mom, etc. but whatever title they call me I feel so blessed and honored. I have asked my extended children if I had done anything wrong or if they thought I had done anything wrong. I have asked them to please forgive me because it is time to forgive and walk in the love of God – real genuine love.

My sweet husband is at peace and rest. His/our daughter, my dear Larsena and I had a good talk a year before she passed – a good loving talk. I thank the Lord we had this talk. God is so good. Her death really got to me. I know by the Holy Spirit she is with her parents, family, friends and other loved ones in heaven waiting on us. What a great reunion that will be, when we all get together in heaven.

I have subsequently had a meeting with some of his children and we all forgave each other.

I lost the love of my life. When you lose the love of your life whether it is caused by death, dementia, by other people encouraging him with the wrong information or just his/her being down right mean it is heartbreaking. However you lose that love there are no words in the dictionary to adequately express your feelings. So we pray for ourselves, the love of our life and for the others that are involved and by all means forgive. That's the greatest gift we can give ourselves… forgiveness.

XXIV

This Far By Faith

I enjoyed going to church. My grandparents had taken me to church when I was a little girl. I enjoyed the singing and how happy the people seemed when they were in church. When we moved to Greenwood, the second home we lived in, at 538 Hackett Street, had a church, right behind the house, on Baptist Street.

My mother and father did not attend, so I started going alone. I enjoyed the feeling of a close knit church family. There was so much genuine love and acceptance shown to me. I felt good there. My brother Joe came with me sometimes but did not enjoy it as much as I did.

Reverend H.B. Mitchell baptized me when I was twelve years old. I became a member of Morris Chapel Baptist Church. I was assistant secretary of the church, an usher and member of the sunshine band. This was before I married.

After Deacon Brown and I married I joined the young adult choir and became superintendent of the Intermediate Sunday school class. My husband was co-chairman of the deacon board and mid-week director of bible study and prayer service. Harry sang in the young people's choir and played football. Ojetta sang in the children's choir and was in the Brownies and girl scouts. I was a Girl Scout leader. We were very active and busy.

After Cherry's death, my mother would often sob so loudly in church on Sundays. Most members thought she should have stayed at home. Her high pitched mournful cries would be heart wrenching. After Sunday school Ojetta would run over to my mother's house. (My mother lived across the street from the church.) If mother was getting ready for church, Ojetta would run back to the church and tell her daddy her stomach was hurting. He would take her home because my mother's loud sobbing was not good for Ojetta's nerves.

When I was at church I had to take care of mother when she began to wail and tend to my child's upset stomach. Often sitting on my other side was the aunt of the man who had hit and killed my sister and his girlfriend. She was crying too. I had my hands full. One Sunday I asked one of the ushers to help me. She was helpful. She stated she was glad to assist me. The ushers at Morris Chapel Baptist Church, where we were members, did their jobs well. While writing this, you know, I realized that I never tended to my own pain. So busy taking care of others. But it has come out in other ways. In ailments and accidents and various diagnosis. My body has held and expressed my pain. I wouldn't advise anyone to take this route. I've learned it's important to Give yourself permission to feel your OWN pain and CRY when you feel like crying!

I was called to preach by God in 1979! I was married to David Edmunds at that time. One day I was coming from Greenwood on my lunch hour. I was working for the Department of Health and Environmental Control.

This family had rented my house on Weldon Street that my first husband Norman and I had lived in. Each month the tenant would put the rent into my account. The hot water heater had gone out so I had gone to purchase a new one. On the way back to my office I began to sing the song, "Go Preach My Gospel."

I asked myself why I kept singing that song. I heard the answer from the Holy Spirit, "Because this is what I want you to do." I ignored the message completely. This was not going to happen. I did not tell anyone. I did not want to think about it. I sure did not want to talk about it.

We had a revival in our town. During the revival the speaker for the week was Dr. David Harrison from Detroit, MI – a dynamic speaker. Dr. Harrison was our pastor's (Rev. Albert Bell) uncle. Pastor Bell was our pastor. His wife was a minister also. That night Dr. Harrison called people up to pray for others. I went up to pray especially for my daughter Ojetta who was in college.

As I returned to my seat the pastor called for people who needed prayer for themselves. I decided not to go to the front again but to kneel where I was. I asked the Lord to come in to my heart. The Lord was already in my heart but I wanted a closer walk with God. I told the Lord I wanted to get as close to Him as I possibly could.

The next week is when I heard the voice of the Lord, as I turned off highway 72 west going towards Abbeville, on my way back to my office at DHEC. I was turning on the old Abbeville Highway. After hearing this voice it seems to me that I just went out into space. I did not discuss this with anyone.

That weekend my daughter came home from college. She and I were talking about the goodness of the Lord. She stated "Mama, sometimes I feel like the Lord wants me to preach." I said, "You are right, when God was speaking to me, it must have been for me to tell you." She said "Ohhhh no. When the message is for me, He will speak to me himself." I said Okay this is not working. Later in her life, the Lord did call Ojetta to preach and she became an ordained minister.

Later the next week I called my brother Bishop Emanuel Spearman and asked him to meet me at the steakhouse in Greenwood. I told him that the Lord had called me to preach. He was excited. I told him I wanted him to help me pray that the Lord would take this "calling" off me. I told him I did not want to preach.

He said "Sis, the Lord will not do that. He called you to preach and you must preach." Then he went on to tell me things that happened to him because he did not want to preach either and he kept saying no to the Lord. He did not want that to happen to me.

I kept saying Lord Give me another sign, another word so that I can be sure that it is really God speaking to me. I knew it was God the first time. I heard his voice. I would go to sleep and the voice would wake me up saying "Go preach the Gospel! Go preach the Gospel!" This went on for about a year.

My husband David would say to me "Lillian, when are you going to preach?" I told him I was not going to preach. I told him to go and preach. He said he had not been called but I had. I told him again that I was not going to preach. He told me that I was supposed to.

I finally called my pastor and told him. He was elated. He said he had been praying for the Lord to call someone to preach in the church and he had been praying for it to be a woman. I wondered why he had done that and why was I chosen?

Some people were not so happy due to their belief that God does not call a woman to preach. According to them, "Women are not supposed to preach". They believe women are supposed to be silent in the church. They can sing, teach Sunday school and hold other positions in the church. I used to hear this when other women were being called into the ministry. I even used to believe that also.

When God called me, then I knew it was for real – that God DID call women as well as men. I was in the A.M.E. church and my pastor Rev. Bell was very supportive as was his wife Sister Bell. We had one pastor after him that did not accept women preachers.

My husband wanted to know why that pastor and I weren't getting along. I told him it was not me, he did not accept my calling from God. My husband David offered to have a talk with him. After he left we had another pastor, Rev. Black, who was very supportive and appreciated my assistance. I need to add under the leadership of Rev. Albert Bell, I accepted Jesus Christ as my Lord and Savior.

One Sunday my husband and I were telling Rev. Bell that we did not see anything wrong about going out on Friday and Saturday night partying and dancing. The next few Sundays we had the same discussion. Rev. Bell talked to us about it again. My husband David said "I don't see anything wrong with it. Do you Lillian?" I said "I don't know." He said "You don't know?" I answered, "I'm not sure." David shrugged his shoulders and said "Oh well!"

I was wearing makeup then but in a few week I was not wearing makeup at all. I had no desire to wear makeup. I felt that maybe makeup was a type of god. Later on I learned that it was okay to wear makeup in moderation.

I was president of the ushers. We were getting new uniforms so we had a meeting with the pastor and his wife. I, along with others, had a pattern to show at the meeting for consideration. My pattern had a slit on each side and strings in the shoulders. The pastor's wife saw the pattern and said the ushers were not supposed to look sexy. I asked her to let her husband, the pastor, see the pattern. He went on worse than his wife saying it was too sexy. I told them it was not sexy! I asked myself what was wrong with these people. Looking back I must admit that pattern was too sexy for ushers.

I finally said "YES" to the Lord and began studying for my first sermon. In the Baptist faith it is called the Trial Sermon. In the A.M.E. church it is called the initial sermon.

One day my husband's brother-in-law, Rev. Henry Smith, called me. He was a pastor and had every book I needed to study. At the same time I was building up my own collection of books I would need. He called to tell me that the founder of a bible college in Columbia, SC was coming to Abbeville to teach bible classes twice a week. He wanted to know if I was interested. Of course I was. I told him I would discuss it with my husband.

My office hours, at work, were from 8:30 AM to 5:00 PM. The bible class ran from 7 PM to 9 PM. I did that for a while. Sometimes I would visit someone until the time for the bible class to begin. When the doctor from the bible college got into the study of homosexuality I could no longer attend the class. This was more than thirty years ago. I did not want to hear anything about the subject at that time.

Being called to preach, when I am by nature very shy, was quite hard. I also stuttered. The Holy Spirit reminded me that Moses stuttered too. Moses thought he could not do what he was called to do either. But in Ex: 4.10 God told him he could. Moses was 83 at the time!

As you know I accepted my calling and did lots of studying. I did my initial sermon in September, 1980. Two of my friends, Sister Ethel Davis and Sister Azalea Cowan's, made me a satin champagne colored robe trimmed in gold. It was beautiful. They surprised me with it. My friends and family from Greenwood, SC; Augusta, GA; Edgefield, SC; and, of course, Calhoun Falls, SC attended. There was a very long line of cars traveling with us to the church. I felt as though I was going to my own funeral. My sermon was from II Timothy.

I had Rev. R. H. Hampton to do the Sermonic Hymn "Go Preach My Gospel." I had his wife Rev. Janie Hampton to read the scripture. The pastor Rev. Albert Bell was presiding. When I walked into the pulpit, I had this surge of heat to come over me. I thought, "This is real. I will never be the same again." Ojetta came home from college. She had just turned nineteen. She was very happy for me. Glovers A.M.E. church was full of people that day.

I had cooked a lot of food. The family and friends were coming back to my home to eat. I had cooked turkey, ham, roast, green beans, turnip greens (fresh from the freezer), macaroni & cheese, potato salad, rice & gravy and fresh tomatoes from the garden. My husband David made sweet potato pies. We also had pound cake, sock-it-to-me cake, coconut pies and lemon meringue pie for desert.

We had a lot of people come over and lots of good food. We were used to having the pastors and their families to dinner after church services, to Christmas dinner and other occasions. I enjoyed it all and so did my family.

I enjoyed cooking and entertaining. I was happy to see people enjoying my food. My first husband, Norman Brown, always told me he had never seen anyone enjoy their own food as much as I did. My initial sermon was beautiful. I felt so loved and blessed.

My ministry began to flourish after leaving David Edmunds for many reasons. Because I had not consulted God about my marriage to Edmunds, there were many stressors in our relationship. Once I left that relationship, they were no longer there and I could focus more fully on my calling. I was able to use more of my energy for evangelizing and counseling. I felt better physically and accepted more invitations to preach.

My ministry is really a ministry of reconciliation and restoration. Because of what I went through as a child and as a young wife, I have a special calling and anointing to counsel those who have been abused or are in abusive relationships.

I love all children. I strongly believe that they should be loved and protected. Blended families, who have difficulty treating all of the children with love and kindness, are another area that I am strong in counseling to positive effects.

My passion is to bring people back together, all people, especially couples and young people, if at all possible.

One of my gifts is teaching them how relationships can be restored. I believe there is a thin line between reconciliation (to be reconciled, to come back into agreement) and restoration (to be brought back to a former state before there was any offense or harm, to be made whole).

My ministry is to couples, individuals and young people. I help them come back into a place of harmony and agreement with one another through honesty, understanding, forgiveness, mercy and love.

Individuals are brought back into a state of spiritual wholeness. I think a lot about young people and I talk to them often, always stressing the importance of education. I stress education because with a good education you can contribute more to society. There is so much struggle involved with no ability to advance oneself. I simply cannot express it strongly enough – education, education, education!

I also talk to young people about not using drugs and alcohol so that they can keep their minds clear and sober. I know my grandchildren, the youth in the church and in the community get tired of hearing me talk about education, being kind and considerate to one another and staying away from drugs. But they know that's what I am going to talk about, so they know what to expect.

Many young people come to me to talk about issues they can't talk to anyone else about. I have seen their hearts and minds be changed. I love allowing God to use me to encourage, educate and strengthen others.

XXV

What Made Me the Woman I am Today

When I look back over my life, I am reminded that I was born poor, ugly and fat. I was born into poverty.

As I stated earlier, in my youth I could see my first cousins, the affluent ones, dressing fashionably. Their homes had nicer furniture. Their parents drove newer cars.

I was thinking all the time, when I grew up, I would get a good education, get married and have children, they would not be raised in a poor environment. I believed that my husband would be a good Christian man. If he loved God, he would love me and our family.

When Deacon Brown asked me to marry him, I felt in my heart he was the husband for me. He had taken good care of his ailing wife for more than three years. He was intelligent, kind and ambitious. On top of that, he was tall and handsome. He convinced me he was the one for me. That he would put God first and his family before himself.

That he did! We did not lack for anything. He was a generous man, Thank the Lord! He went shopping for me. Many days I came home from work and he had clothes lying on the guest room bed for me to try on. I did the same for him. He did the same with jewelry. He knew the things I liked.

One day he surprised me with a lovely chandelier. He had someone put it up in the living room before I came home. Another time he surprised me with a new car – an Oldsmobile.

He and I shopped for our children. He did not like to shop with me. I could go from store to store looking and deciding. My husband would have his mind made up and go to one store, or maybe two, and purchase what he had decided on. He would say, "Sugar babe, you take this money and go shopping for the children when you want to."

I'm proud to say that the Lord was our Shepherd and we did not want for anything. Praise his name!!

I did a lot for my mother, too! I wanted her to enjoy some of the nicer things in life. She used to tell me, "You are so good to me!"

My children were told and knew early in life that an education is the key to advancing in the world and creating opportunities for themselves and others to live an abundant life. I am now telling my grandchildren the same thing!

Earlier in life as I babysat for the Crymes and the Daniels, they had beautiful homes with elegant furniture, plush drapes and carpet. Coming from where I had come from, I had never seen nor had I even imagined that people could live that way. I declared to myself and claimed, right then and there, "I will have this one day!" I knew that one day, I would have a beautiful home and a peaceful loving family.

Being a part of their families, opened my imagination and helped me to dream. Never underestimate the power of your imagination or the power of your dreams. Never underestimate your power to positively impact the life of a child. When you set your heart and mind toward accomplishing something, set that as a goal, and work towards it; if you don't give up, you will accomplish it.

I have three mottos. The first is: "Do unto others as you would have them do unto you!" The second one is: "I can do all things through Christ who strengthens me", and the third one is: "I am blessed to be a blessing."

I cannot say one motto is more important. I think they are all equally important. To me, God and education go hand in hand. Of course, God is Number One – first and foremost, then education. Then, when you are blessed, always remember to give something back; bless others.

Accept Jesus in your life, then seek for directions concerning your career and life. We all have different talents, gifts, callings and the things we enjoy in life. Mine is nursing, counseling, and being a mother.

I am a mother to many children. I had two of my own and two through marriage. I don't like the term stepmother. I also have several god children. Others I have adopted or are my spiritual children, my God children.

I love all my children as if I had given birth to them. I could never hurt them in any fashion, only love and nurture them. I love them/you all so much and God loves you more!

Some of my children are close to me in age while some are actually older than I am. The age does not matter. It is not about the biological relationship but the love in your heart. I am honored to be called Mother Washington, to be called an extension of your own mother.

My "children" call me Mama, Mother and Mom. What they call me doesn't matter, whatever title they have given me as their "Mother" I am proud.

But it all began with those first three little lives the Lord entrusted in my care and who lovingly called me Mama – My dear sons Harry, Willie James and my beloved daughter Ojetta.

I have tried to give my children genuine and honest counseling and direction with love, bearing in mind what is unique about each one of them. My children and grandchildren are all very gifted and creative in their own ways. Each has found or is finding their path.

My grandson Darius is an internet whiz and very creative. My granddaughter Cherry enjoys photography and design. My granddaughter Ebony has a gift for praise dancing and wants to be a mortician.

I had low self-esteem most of my growing up years. I began to feel better about myself when I was approximately 16 years old. I realized at that age that I was going to work for what I wanted in life and what I deserved. I also wanted a good life for my little sister Cherry.

She was married at age 15. I tried to tell her to get her education. She told me she would get it later. The Holy Spirit knew she did not have long on the earth. She was killed in an auto accident at age 19. Had she not followed her internal knowing and married early I would not have had my niece and nephew, Ivey Irene and Norman (Chip) Thompson Jr., to help raise and enjoy. At the time of Cherry's death Ivey was one year old and chip was 2 ½ years old.

During my sister's short life, I did a lot to make her life comfortable as well as my mother's and others. I only wish I had had more time with them; yet, I do not regret how I have treated any of my family members who were taken too soon. I loved them with all my heart while they were here and I believed that I showed them by my actions. It is so important to be kind to those who you love and show them as often as you can that you care. Tomorrow is not promised to us and I try not to take those I love for granted. I have taught my children that. "To Love as best you can, while you can."

I have written this book to encourage others to confront, address and process their pain. Because I did not address and process my pain while I was going through it, it has led to many health issues.

I've been through a lot; I'm still processing different aspects of the pain I've experienced in my life. With each layer of pain that I peel back, process and let go, I am getting lighter and healthier.

I have written this book to encourage others to pray and not minimize the hard experiences they go through. Feel your pain, talk about it and allow others to help you.

Aftermath

In October 2008, my daughter Ojetta wrote me a letter stating that the Holy Spirit had directed her to tell me that, "We are blessed and highly favored, throughout the Heavens and the earth, and that is God's continual command for me and my lineage!"

In 2008, I was blessed with the most wonderful "caregiving" position. They were Christians first and foremost. I would not work for non-Christians. (I was at the point in my life that I could make that decision.) They were a joy to care for.

I started on the third shift. There was a lady on the first and another on the second shift. One day we had a meeting. The man of the house (husband), asked me if I thought they needed care at night. Everyone looked at me.

I told him I didn't think a third shift was necessary at all because he and his wife slept all night. The other care givers thought I had just talked myself out of a job or was trying to get the first shift. I did not want the second shift, maybe to fill in at times, but not full time.

I strongly believe, "Honesty is the best policy." So I had to pray and think about how I was going to decide between first and second shifts. Everyone was panicking in the house not knowing what was going to happen.

The husband had asked me to be in charge of the schedules and making out the time sheets for payment. The caregiver on the first shift thought I was going to eliminate her position but I couldn't fairly do that. So I asked her if we could split her shift.

She would have four days a week and I would have three then we would switch days the next week. She said she would be fine if she had three days a week because she was grateful I didn't take all of the days. I told her I could not treat her that way. My motto is "do unto others as you would have them do unto you."

That worked so well. We all got along like family. I enjoyed being with them until I fell and had a closed head injury.

One afternoon, while shopping, I slipped on a loose rug when entering the store and hit my head. I had fluid (swelling) at the back of my brain, which made thinking and making decisions very difficult. I was often confused and it was difficult to distinguish between similar things or understand simple things. My memory was affected, I began to understand what my sweet husband, Alfred Washington, had gone through. For a while I actually forgot about my last two husbands and my thoughts went back to my first husband, Norman Brown. Then, I could understand Washington's mind going back to his first wife. We often can't understand what we have not experienced. That was quite an experience for me. God showed me how it could happen.

I knew I needed help, not just physically, but emotionally. I got a therapist, Dr. Katina Wright. Evangelist Clark had driven me to her office for my first few visits. The first time my daughter Shirley drove me to my therapist, I could not tell her the way. We kept going up and down the highway. I did not know where I was going, nothing looked familiar. We had to call the psychologist to get the directions. We were late for the appointment but the therapist understood. She was so nice, kind and professional. I learned that Dr. Wright had passed September 9, 2014. I was sorry to hear this. She was a phenomenal counselor and helped me a lot. Over time, she became my friend.

During that time, I would hear voices and things falling. I never knew how many parts of the brain are affected by a closed head injury. It was a terrible time for me but again help from family, friends and church family was a blessing to me. This condition lasted on and off for about a year and a half. I thank the Lord that as I write this on February 20, 2015 I have for the most part recovered. Thank you Jesus!

Things can happen so quickly! Through it all God is so good. I am thankful it wasn't any worse. Everyday trusting God for the next day! God is our true provider! He makes a way when it seems there isn't one. Of course, we know he is the way, the truth and the life. We know He is always present. Yet when we feel we are alone, God makes His presence known in a sweet and powerful way! Every time!

XXVII

Epilogue

In the beginning of this book I expressed how I was beat up in the womb because my mother did not want me. I thought my mother beat me in real life because she did not love me. I have learned through life's journey it was not about me at all. My mother had the problem. My mother was depressed and sick and feeling unloved herself. She took her pain out on me, her husband, my little brother, my little sister, and everyone she came in contact with, but mainly herself. She was in a lot of pain and she inflicted a lot of pain. I prayed for my mother, but when I became an adult, I did not allow her to inflict the same pain on my little sister. Overtime, miraculously she changed. I didn't know how the change had occurred. I just knew that she had changed and before she died, I had a sweet mother. On August 7, 2015 at 5:19 PM, while reading over my story, the Holy Spirit revealed the answer, "Your mother was Bi-polar. It was never diagnosed or treated. One day, I miraculously healed her." Thank you Jesus!

My first husband, Norman Brown, had to deal with the affair he had while married to his first wife. HE had to deal with the feelings of guilt and depression that he felt. His feelings affected our family, he drank too much and was mean, wrestling with his conscience. I did not point fingers at him or judge him. I encouraged him to forgive himself and I also prayed for his healing and strength. Who are we to judge anyway? Yea, let him who is without sin cast the first stone! I'm sure those feelings affected my husband's health. When we ask for forgiveness, we have to be willing to forgive ourselves.

When we, my husband Norman and I, got pregnant before marriage we did not spend a lot of time regretting the pregnancy. I always wanted marriage first and then the children. I think I was more ashamed of the act; but, we repented immediately and asked the Lord to forgive us. We did not ever discuss it again because we knew at that point we were back in the righteousness of God! If you miss the mark, don't worry, don't fret! Repent quickly and get it right with God, in Jesus name!

Excessive drinking caused problems in our marriage! Drinking helped him to cope with his unspoken feelings of guilt and sadness. Even though he loved his family, my husband Norman was not able to stop drinking until he could talk about what was tormenting his soul. I'm glad I was able to encourage him to talk about what was bothering him. It was not easy for him, or me; yet, he knew that if he didn't talk about the issues and stop drinking, I was going to leave. Trying to cover over a problem with drinking, drugs, overeating, gambling, addictive behavior, even excessive shopping will not make the problem go away; it only causes more problems. There comes a time when you have to get your priorities in order and do whatever it takes to save your life and that of your family.

My first child Harry was such a gift to me. His big brown eyes, bright smile and sweet spirit melted my heart before his father and I got married. When he first called me "Mama," it was true in every way. Being his mother brought out a love and the maternal instinct that would make it impossible for me to love him any less or treat him any differently than any child that I gave birth to. I had to defend him against my husband who sometimes insensitively compared him to others. Harry was a gentle, intelligent, talented little soul who grew into a strong man. My love for and pride in my son made it important for me to counsel blended families and rebuke parents who referred to any of their children as "step" children. My relationship with my son shaped my ability to be a loving mother and a friend. Our son Harry lives in Florida with his wife Virginia O. Brown. Harry helped Virginia to rear her two children Greg and Pam. He deeply loved and treated them like his children. He remembered the love expressed in our home and how he was raised. He told me, "I remember how you loved me Mama." Pam and Greg love him as their father. Harry found a loving and devoted wife who is doing an excellent job of caring for him since he suffered a severe stroke in January, 2009. He was also diagnosed with cancer 2 years later. Virginia and I speak several times a month via the phone. Though he cannot speak and is wheelchair bound he can hold the phone and indicate he understands what is said to him by grunts and Belly laughs. Though his body is affected, his mind and loving spirit are still intact.

Ojetta's birth was a blessing to the whole family – She was so sweet and darling. She was an old soul. I learned so much from my daughter, even when she was a little girl, she would speak with such wisdom. We knew she was a special gift from God to us. In some ways we grew up together. Even though, as a parent, you are your children's first teacher never underestimate what your children can teach you. Be open to seeing their special gifts and talents, that they have, and encourage them in what's truly best for them. Allow God to show you their own beautiful uniqueness, because they all have that. Don't be selfish and insist that they do things your way, forsaking what God has put in them. Don't force your children to be something that they're not just to make you happy. As you love them and encourage them to thrive and be themselves they will love themselves and know how to love others. They will be able to make wise decisions and fulfill their reason for being born. God knows the purpose and why he creates each child, we don't. Allow God to do His own perfect work in and through your child. Ojetta's honesty and courage in standing firm in, how God made her has taught me this. It wasn't easy in the beginning, but I love my child. God taught me how to be a better parent and how to truly love unconditionally. Ojetta is passionate about her life and helping others be healthier and passionate about theirs. She has had her own health issues, but has sought help. She is committed to be healthier every day. She is in a loving relationship and has her own Wellness business; empowering people to be healthy physically, spiritually, and emotionally.

My son Willie James was born and died thirteen months later. He died from meningitis after being hospitalized for over two weeks. What a sweet and joyous soul he was. It felt so unfair to have a child just one year and then, when he has your whole heart, to have to let him go. Losing a child is the hardest thing a couple can go through. No words can express the depth of that pain. No words. Many couples who have lost a child don't make it. Looking back…. I'm surprised our marriage lasted because the death of a child completely shatters you. You're the same people, but at the same time, you're really not. Everyone changes throughout the course of a marriage, but it's rarely so sudden and complete as after the death of a child. So we really had to get to know each other again in one of the most harrowing circumstances imaginable. We still had our struggles, and, as anyone who's suffered loss can tell you, you never know what life is going to throw at you. We didn't talk about our son's death. I hadn't learned how to grieve, in a healthy way, and he didn't know how either. We focused on Harry, Ojetta, and ourselves and not on what could have been or might be coming. It was hard. Very hard.

I have since then learned that people grieve differently. No two people grieve the same, even when they're grieving the same loss. But when you have a partner, you *do* have someone who understands, and it's both a blessing and a curse. A blessing not to have to walk the path alone. A curse because some days it's all you can do is to help *yourself* survive, let alone someone else. If I had known better, I would have sought grief counseling with my husband or alone which ever suited our comfort level. If you have lost a child, please get some help to share your pain and your feelings. You will be healthier and happier for it in the long run.

My sister Cherry Oglesby-Thompson was killed August 28, 1972, two days after her nineteenth birthday. This was a time that went from great celebration to utter disbelief.... We were too shocked to really respond. I thought so many times that her children and husband, Norman, could have been killed too. In spite of losing my sister, I would think sometimes, God is still good because the entire family could have been killed! Overall, everybody was walking around in shock and were extremely sad.

Three months later, on December 1, 1972, my husband Norman Brown died suddenly! The rug was totally snatched out from under me, Ojetta and Harry and we were like dead people walking around. Still breathing but not living. We buried him and continued with our day to day activities. Again not talking about what we were feeling, each of us crying alone and feeling depressed. I honestly don't know how they finished school. I don't know how I did what I had to do every day. It had to be the power and grace of God. My children knew God and they knew how to pray, but if I knew what I know today, I would have made sure that we were talking to each other and seeing a counselor to help us deal with the trauma and tremendous amount of pain and sadness we were feeling. There are so many ways and places to get grief counseling today. Talk to your doctor, a counselor, a social worker. Google "grief counseling" in your area and get the help you need. Don't suffer like we did.

My zombie walk continued and intensified as my mother's illness required me to attend to her. I am certain that my mother's emotional state contributed to her physical illness and early death. She didn't talk about symptoms that she had been experiencing until it was too late. Please ladies, if you have gone through menopause and start having any vaginal bleeding go to the Dr. right away. That could be a symptom of something serious, like uterine cancer, as it was in my mother's case. My mother died a horrible slow death at 54 years of age. Back then the treatment was worse than the disease. Burning hot Cobalt inserted into the vagina. Suffice it to say, it was terrible. I kept going. Didn't stop to think about it, didn't cry, didn't complain, just did what I needed to do to try to make her my mother's life comfortable until she died.

Didn't really stop to take a breath, married David Edmunds, he had walked with me through hell, while caring for my mother. So what if he was a flirt!?! He had been so thoughtful and helpful to me. I was just tired. I tried to justify why I married him, but really, when you are so exhausted and beat down by stress and caring for others, it seems like any port in a storm will do. Well, I learned otherwise. Don't make an important decision when you're bone tired and heart weary. You aren't thinking clearly. Don't make any decisions when you haven't consulted God. You will regret it. That marriage ended in divorce.

I moved on my own and reconnected to the God of my understanding, Jesus Christ. I came to realize that I had been taking care of everybody but myself. I realized that I had not loved myself as much as I had loved others. I realized that I had to start pampering me and taking good care of me. I had to love myself in order for true love to come to me. I started exercising and eating better, reading inspirational and self-help books. I started really meditating on the scriptures that I had been reading. In all my decisions, I did not move until I consulted the Lord. I realized that I am truly a Queen and deserved the best in every area of my life. I met and Married the Love of my Life, Alfred Washington. Initially, some of his children did not like me. It was hard dealing with their disapproval and negative energy, but I loved my husband. And I forgave them. (In 2016, a heartfelt meeting with his children resulted in true healing and forgiveness, which confirms my faith and belief that it's never too late for healing.)

Washington and I were married for fourteen years. After his death, I suffered a closed head injury and finally sought help for my mind and emotions. Many of us are suffering from emotional and mental health problems but would never consider counseling. We have bodies that get weak, get injured, get diseased and hopefully we recognize the importance of getting proper treatment for our bodies. We also have emotions and mental states that get unbalanced that require proper treatment that sometimes includes medication. Why do we prefer to suffer than to go to someone who is trained and experienced to help us in the areas of our minds and our emotions? Why, as Black people, other people too, but especially Black people, feel that if we go to a counselor or therapist it is a sign of weakness or an admission that you are "crazy!?!" We have to get over this dangerous way of thinking! Too many of us are dying from mental health and emotional conditions that most of the time, can easily be diagnosed and treated. Our emotions affect our physical bodies and lives in so many ways. Events (such as childhood trauma, death, divorce, physical abuse, abandonment, etc.) that we experience, affect our emotions and then our bodies. It's ok to feel down for a while, but if you can't seem to bounce back and you are struggling to find peace more days than not – talk to a qualified counselor and check in, just to see if they can help you. Don't wait until you are in the pit of depression and too sick or too tired to move. Depression makes you tired. Depression makes you sick. Let me just break it down to you, Depression kills. Don't suffer for years as I, and so many others, have. Talk to someone about what you're going through. There is hope for you.

Lastly, many people don't understand why I tend to be kind and willing to forgive quickly. They think that my way of being is a weakness. But, I have learned, and God has confirmed it for me; that being unkind, worrying and holding grudges make you weak and you still don't get the results you desire. God told me that, 'Prayer, not worry, is my weapon' and that 'He would handle it' (fight my battles for me.) You know, I believe that. And every day I trust God to do exactly what He has said. Focusing on God's Goodness keeps my Love and forgiveness flowing. It also keeps God's Love and Forgiveness flowing towards me. The Joy of the Lord is my strength……. Because I have come this far, by faith!

I hope this book helps you to see how YOU can go through the fire and come out as pure gold!!

Acknowledgements

To my parents: Jimmy Joe Oglesby and Lillie Lou Bush Oglesby, thank you for being the best parents you knew how to be. I LOVE YOU!!

To my Siblings: Joe Edward Oglesby, Bishop Emanuel Spearman, Cherry Oglesby Thompson (deceased), Jimmy Lagroom Oglesby, and Effie Turner. I LOVE YOU!!

To my daughters: Rev. Lillian Ojetta Brown, Michelle E. Brown and Connie Jenkins Piper. Thank you for your loyal support and for being my teachers. Your contribution to this book has been enormous and I am eternally grateful for your time, love and dedication. I LOVE YOU!!

To my daughter Ivey Sanders who continued to say, "Mother, it's time to write your book!" I LOVE YOU!!

To all my children, God children, grandchildren and spiritual children:

Harry Brown, Willie James Brown (deceased), Shirley Ann Cunningham, Desima White, Deacon Herbert Barnes (deceased), Huey White.

Darius R. Martin, Cherry S. Martin, Ebony Brianna Oglesby Sanders, T-Shae Sanders.

Robert Allen, Darryl Bell Jr., Lessa T. Washington, Sanquinetta S. Williams, Betty Arlene Dubose. I LOVE YOU ALL!!

To My Faithful Friends:

Irene Peterson Gordon (deceased), Julia Mae Holliday, Viola Louden Carroll, Mary Moss, Minister Georgia East, Evangelist Fannie Clark, Pearl Blair Aiken, Willie Cornelia Reid, Betty W. Singleton, Azalee Cowan, Evangelist Gladys Wardlaw, Diana Dubose - Baskin, Alice Brown, Dr. Sallie Tate and Sarah Butler (deceased). Thank you for your tried and true friendship. I LOVE YOU!!

To my Adopted Families:

Dr. and Mrs. John F. Daniels, Mary G. Daniel-Wyatt, John Daniel (deceased), Lambert and Russel Daniel.

Mr. and Mrs. Neil Crymes, Park Crymes, Harriett Crymes and Neil Crymes Jr. (Buster- deceased).

Thank you for embracing me as a part of your own family! I LOVE YOU!!

Printed in the United States
By Bookmasters